C++
Essentials

T0383994

A Wiley Brand

C++
Essentials

by John Paul Mueller

EDITED BY **Ronald Mak**

C++ Essentials For Dummies®

Published by: **John Wiley & Sons, Inc.**, 111 River Street, Hoboken, NJ 07030-5774, www.wiley.com

For general information on our other products and services, please contact our Customer Care Department within the U.S. at 877-762-2974, outside the U.S. at 317-572-3993, or fax 317-572-4002. For technical support, please visit https://hub.wiley.com/community/support/dummies.

Wiley publishes in a variety of print and electronic formats and by print-on-demand. Some material included with standard print versions of this book may not be included in e-books or in print-on-demand. If this book refers to media such as a CD or DVD that is not included in the version you purchased, you may download this material at http://booksupport.wiley.com. For more information about Wiley products, visit www.wiley.com.

Library of Congress Control Number is available from the publisher.

ISBN 978-1-394-30788-3 (pbk); ISBN 978-1-394-30790-6 (ebk); ISBN 978-1-394-30789-0 (ebk)

SKY10093229_120624

Contents at a Glance

Table of Contents

Introduction

Welcome to *C++ Essentials For Dummies*. This book contains the basic information you need to know to get going with C++ programming. You'll learn how to install and run the compiler, write programs, and use important C++ features like arrays, classes, and pointers to do good object-oriented programming.

C++ is a large and complex language. But whether you're just learning to program or you're an expert in other programming languages, this book contains the essentials of the language for you to quickly become a C++ programmer.

About This Book

C++ Essentials For Dummies contains the information you need to start writing C++ programs. You can compile and run the example programs with the latest C++ 20 version of the compiler, but you can also use the earlier C++ 14 and C++ 17 versions.

This book is not a comprehensive reference for C++. To go beyond what this book covers, your next book should be *C++ All-in-One For Dummies*, 4th Edition by John Paul Mueller, from which this book is derived. However, this book will get you up and running fast with its easy-to-follow *For Dummies* format.

Foolish Assumptions

We made a few basic assumptions about you, the reader:

>> **You own or have access to a relatively modern computer.** The C++ example programs were tested on a Windows computer, but the book shows how to compile and run them just as easily on a Mac or Linux computer.

>> **You're an experienced computer user.** In other words, we assume that you know the basics of using your computer, such as starting programs and working with the file system.

>> **You're interested in learning how to write programs in the C++ language.** That's what this book is about, so it's a fair assumption.

We do *not* assume you have any previous programming experience in C++ or in any other programming language.

Icons Used in This Book

Like any *For Dummies* book, this book is chock-full of helpful icons that draw your attention to items of particular importance. You find the following icons throughout this book:

WARNING

Danger! This icon highlights information that may help you avert disaster.

REMEMBER

Did we tell you about the memory course we took?

TIP

Pay special attention to this icon; it lets you know that some particularly useful tidbit is at hand.

Where to Go from Here

If you're new to programming, you'll benefit most from this book by reading it from start to end. But if you're familiar with programming in another language, especially an object-oriented language like Java, you can pick and choose which chapters and topics to read to learn what's unique about C++.

Chapter **1**

Compiling and Running Your First C++ Application

A C++ compiler translates your source files (which contain the text of your application's program code written in C++) into machine code that your computer can understand and run. Different C++ compilers run on the Microsoft Windows, Apple macOS, and Linux operating systems, but they all adhere to the international standard for C++, so if you write your program code in C++, you should be able to compile and run your application on any of the platforms.

This chapter has links to download and install the C++ compiler on the Windows, macOS, and Linux platforms. It demonstrates how to edit, compile, and run a simple C++ application on the command line (that is, in a terminal window) in each of the platforms.

Then it briefly looks at using an integrated development environment (IDE) and shows you the advantages an IDE offers to C++ developers. Many IDEs are available, so this chapter only gives an introduction to using one. The rest of this book assumes you're compiling and running programs on the command line.

Looking at a Simple C++ Program

Use any text editor (such as Windows Notepad, macOS TextEdit, or Linux vi) to create a plain-text file named hello.cpp containing the following C++ code:

```cpp
#include <iostream>

using namespace std;

int main()
{
    for (int i = 1; i <= 5; i++)
    {
        cout << i << " Hello, world!" << endl;
    }
}
```

Using C++ on Microsoft Windows

On the Windows platform, the C++ compiler is a utility program called CL that you run on the command line in a special command window.

To install CL, follow these steps:

1. **Go to** https://visualstudio.microsoft.com/downloads/#build-tools-for-visual-studio-2022.

2. **Scroll down to Build Tools for Visual Studio and click the Download button.**

   An installer downloads onto your computer.

3. **Run the installer to install CL and its tools.**

You must run CL in a special command window. Left-click the Start button at the bottom of the screen. Scroll down to the Visual Studio 2022 folder, and click the down arrow to the right of the folder to reveal the folder's contents. Left-click Developer Command Prompt for VS 2022 to open a command window especially set up to run CL. On the command line of that window, enter the following command on one line:

```
cl /EHsc /std:c++20 hello.cpp /link /out:hello.exe
```

This command compiles the source file and generates the executable file hello.exe. To run the executable file, enter the following command:

```
hello
```

In later chapters, an application may consist of multiple source files. Then, instead of specifying a single source file like hello. cpp, you would tell CL to compile all the source files in the directory whose names end with .cpp. For example:

```
cl /EHsc /std:c++20 *.cpp /link /out:books.exe
```

These example commands include the /std:c++20 parameter to specify using the standard 2020 version of C++. You should be able compile this book's examples with earlier versions of C++ by specifying /std:c++14 or /std:c++17.

The /link option says that the next option is meant for the *linkage editor*, a tool that combines the output of the compiler into an executable program. The /out parameter tells the linkage editor what to name the executable program.

/EHsc tells the compiler how to generate code to handle exceptions, which are runtime errors. Exception handling is briefly covered in Chapter 9.

TIP

For a walk-through on compiling and running a C++ program on the command line, go to https://learn.microsoft.com/en-us/cpp/build/walkthrough-compiling-a-native-cpp-program-on-the-command-line. For descriptions of the CL compiler options, go to https://learn.microsoft.com/en-us/cpp/build/reference/compiler-options-listed-alphabetically.

Using C++ on Apple macOS

On macOS, you can use the Clang C++ compiler. For instructions on how to install the compiler, go to https://osxdaily.com/2023/05/02/how-install-gcc-mac.

After installing the compiler, go to the folder where you stored your source file, `hello.cpp`, and enter the following command in a Terminal window:

```
g++ -std=c++0x -o hello hello.cpp
```

This command runs the C++ compiler to compile the source file and generates the executable file `hello`. To run the executable file, enter the following command:

```
./hello
```

In later chapters, an application may consist of multiple source files. Then, instead of specifying a single source file like `hello.cpp`, you would tell `g++` to compile all the source files in the directory whose names end with `.cpp`. For example:

```
g++ -std=c++20 -o books *.cpp
```

These example commands include the `-std:c++20` parameter to specify using the standard 2020 version of C++. You should be able compile this book's examples with versions as early as 2011 by specifying `-std=c++11` or `-std=c++0x`. The `-o` parameter gives the name of the executable program.

Using C++ on Linux

On Linux, you can use the GNU C++ compiler. For instructions on how to install the compiler, go to `www.cherryservers.com/blog/how-to-install-gcc-on-ubuntu`.

After installing the compiler, go to the folder where you stored your source file, `hello.cpp`. Enter the following command in a Terminal window:

```
g++ -std=c++20 -o hello hello.cpp
```

This command runs the C++ compiler to compile the source file and generates the application `hello`. To run the executable file, enter the following command:

```
./hello
```

In later chapters, an application may consist of multiple source files. Then, instead of specifying a single source file, like `hello.cpp`, you would tell g++ to compile all the source files in the directory whose names end with `.cpp`. For example:

```
g++ -std=c++20 -o books *.cpp
```

These example commands include the -std:c++20 or -std=c++2a parameter to specify using the standard 2020 version of C++. You should be able compile this book's examples with versions as early as 2011 by specifying -std=c++11 or -std=c++0x). The -o parameter gives the name of the executable program.

Working with an Integrated Development Environment

An IDE is an application that combines a syntax-aware code editor, a compiler, a debugger, and often other tools. Many IDEs are cross-platform — they have versions that run on different platforms. Others only run on particular platforms. Some IDEs for C++ include the following:

>> CLion (cross-platform; www.jetbrains.com/clion)

>> Code::Blocks (cross-platform; www.codeblocks.org)

>> Eclipse CDT (cross-platform; https://projects.eclipse.org/projects/tools.cdt)

>> Microsoft Visual C++ (https://visualstudio.microsoft.com/downloads)

>> Visual Studio (cross-platform; https://visualstudio.microsoft.com)

>> Xcode (Apple macOS; https://developer.apple.com/xcode)

An IDE's syntax-aware code editor makes it easy to edit C++ code. It can use color-coding to highlight different source code components, such as keywords, and flag syntax errors as you type the code.

The debugger has features to help you get your code to run correctly. You can set breakpoints at statements to cause your program to temporarily pause at those statements during execution. When your program is paused at a breakpoint, you can examine the current values of variables. You can *single-step* (execute one statement at a time while you monitor the values of variables), or you can resume normal program execution.

Figure 1-1 shows debugging hello.cpp in Eclipse CDT. The program is paused at the cout statement. You can see that the current value of variable i is 4.

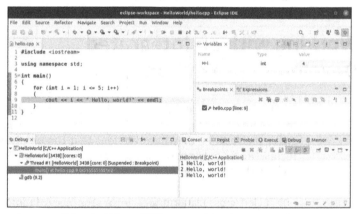

FIGURE 1-1: Using the Eclipse CDT integrated development environment (IDE).

Using an IDE greatly simplifies C++ application development, but how to use an IDE is beyond the scope of this book. If you're interested in learning more, you can find online tutorials for any IDE you want to use.

Chapter **2**

Storing Data in C++

The best way to think of memory is as a set of storage bins. When you write a computer application, you reserve some storage bins, and you give each storage bin a name. You also say what type of thing can be stored in the storage bin. The technical term for such a storage bin is a *variable*.

In this chapter, you discover how you can use these storage bins in your applications.

Storing Values in Variables

When you write an application, you specify that you want to make use of one or more storage bins called *variables*. Each computer storage bin can hold only one value at a time. A variable is simply a storage bin with an associated name.

You can put many different types of values into your variables. For example, you can put numbers in a storage bin, or you can put a string in a storage bin. (However, each storage bin contains a unique kind of data — you can't put a number into a storage bin designed for a string.) As for numbers, they can be either *integers* (which are positive whole numbers, negative whole numbers, and 0) or numbers with a decimal point, such as 3.11 or 10.0, which (for various reasons) are called *floating-point numbers.*

The term *floating-point number* refers to a number that has a decimal point and something to the right of the decimal point (even if it's just a 0). When you see the term *floating point*, you can remember what it means by focusing on the word *point* in its name — when you see *point*, think of decimal point.

Creating an integer variable

In your C++ application, you can easily write a line of code that creates a variable. Although the variable doesn't actually get created until you run the application, people often refer to this process as *creating a variable.* A variable has three aspects:

>> **Name:** Every variable must have a name. In your application, you refer to the variable by this name. For example, you may have a variable called count, and you may have a variable called LastName.

>> **Type:** When you create a variable, you must specify the type of value the variable can hold. For example, one variable may hold an integer, and another variable may hold a single character. After you pick a type for the variable in your application, you can put only values of that type into the variable.

>> **Value:** At any given moment, a simple variable holds a single value. (Chapter 8 describes *array* variables that can hold multiple values.) For example, an integer variable may hold the number 10, and a character variable might hold the character a.

You *declare* a variable when you specify its type and name. That is known as a *variable declaration.*

The code for the SimpleVariable example, shown here, demonstrates how to create a variable:

```cpp
#include <iostream>

using namespace std;

int main()
{
    int mynumber;
    mynumber = 10;
    cout << mynumber << endl;
    return 0;
}
```

This is a full application that you can run.

Take a careful look at this code. Remember that the computer starts with the code inside the braces that follow main(), and it performs the code line by line.

The first line inside main looks like this:

```cpp
int mynumber;
```

When you declare a variable, the first thing you specify is the type of thing the variable can hold. Here, you use the word int. This word is the C++ word for *integer*. Thus, the variable that you're declaring can hold an integer. Next is the name of the variable. This variable is named mynumber. Then a semicolon ends the variable declaration.

The next line looks like this:

```cpp
mynumber = 10;
```

This line puts the value 10 in the variable. Because you already know that the variable can hold an integer, you're allowed to put in a 10 because it's an integer. If you'd tried to put a value other than an integer in the variable, the compiler would've given you an error message. The compiler makes sure that you put into a variable only the same type of value. And, of course, you noticed that the statement ends with a semicolon. In C++, every statement ends with a semicolon.

To put a value in a variable, you type the variable's name, an equal sign (surrounded by optional spaces), and the value. You end the line with a semicolon. This line of code is an *assignment statement*. Or you can say that you're *setting* the variable to the value.

The next line is this:

```
cout << mynumber << endl;
```

This is a cout statement, which means that it writes something on the console. This code tells the computer to write the value of mynumber on the console. The previous line of code put a 10 in the storage bin, so this line prints a 10 on the console. The endl means "end line", so the 10 is printed on a line by itself. When you run the application, you see this:

```
10
```

Think of it like this: When you type the variable's name, you're accessing the variable. The exception to this is when the variable's name appears to the left of an equal sign. In that case, you're setting the variable. You can do two things with a variable:

>> **Setting the variable:** You can set a variable, which means that you can put a value inside the storage bin.

>> **Retrieving the value:** You can get back the value that is inside the variable. When you do so, the value stays inside it.

When you retrieve the value that's in a variable, you aren't removing it from the variable. The value is still inside the variable.

Declaring multiple variables

If you want to declare three integer variables in a row, you can do it in a single declaration statement, like this:

```
int monica, rachel, phoebe;
```

This statement declares three separate variables. The first is called monica; the second is called rachel; and the third is called phoebe. Each of these three variables can have an integer value. You haven't put anything in any of them, so you may follow that with some code to assign each of them a value. For example, this code puts the value 10 in monica, 20 in rachel, and 3254 in phoebe.

```
monica = 10;
rachel = 20;
phoebe = 3254;
```

When you run your applications, the computer executes the statements in the order in which they appear in your code. Therefore, in the preceding code, the computer first creates the three storage bins. Then it puts the value 10 inside monica. Next, rachel gets the value 20. And finally, phoebe gets the value 3254.

Changing values

Although a variable can hold only one value at a time, you can still change what the variable holds. After you put another value in a variable, it forgets what it originally had.

You put another value in the variable in the same way you originally put a value in it. Look closely at the code for the ChangeVariable example:

```
#include <iostream>

using namespace std;

int main()
{
    int mynumber;
    mynumber = 10;
    cout << mynumber << endl;

    mynumber = 20;
    cout << mynumber << endl;
    return 0;
}
```

When you see a single equal sign by itself, the item on the left side is the variable item that receives the value that is on the right side.

Setting one variable equal to another

Because you can do only two direct things with variables — put something in and retrieve the value — setting one variable equal to another is a simple process of retrieving the value of one variable and putting it in the other. This process is often referred to as *copying* the variable from one to another. For example, if you have two integer variables — say, start and finish — and you want to copy the value of start into finish, you would use a line of code like the following:

```
finish = start;
```

WARNING

Don't let the language confuse you. Although you want to copy the value of start into finish, notice that the first thing you type is **finish**, and then the equal sign, and then **start**. The left side of the equal sign is what *receives* the value.

REMEMBER

When you copy the value of one variable to another, the two variables must be the same type. For instance, you can't copy the value from a string variable into an integer variable. If you try, the compiler issues an error message.

After the computer runs this copy statement, the two variables hold the same value. The code for CopyVariable, shown here, is an example of copying the value from one variable to another:

```
#include <iostream>

using namespace std;

int main()
{
    int start = 50;
    int finish;
    finish = start;
    cout << finish << endl;
    return 0;
}
```

Initializing a variable

When you create a variable, it starts as an empty storage bin. But before it can be of much use, you need to put a value in it.

If you try to retrieve the contents of a variable before you actually put a value in it, you end up with what computer people fondly call "unpredictable results." So, always make sure that you place a value inside a variable before you try to retrieve its contents, a process called *initializing the variable.*

You can initialize a variable in two ways. The first way is by declaring the variable and then assigning something into it, which takes two lines of code:

```
int mynumber;
mynumber = 153;
```

But the other way is a bit quicker. It looks like this:

```
int mynumber = 153;
```

This method combines both strategies into one neat little package that is available for you to use whenever you want. You see variables initialized both ways in this book.

Creating a great name for yourself

Every variable needs to have a name. But what names can you use? Although you're free to use names such as Fred, Zanzibar, or Supercount1000M, there are limits to what C++ will allow you to use.

Although most C++ code is in lowercase, you're free to use upper-case letters in your variable names. However, C++ distinguishes between the two. The compiler treats the two names as two different variables, which makes C++ case-sensitive.

Here are the rules you need to follow when creating a variable name:

>> **Characters:** You can use any uppercase letter, lowercase letter, number, or underscore in your variable names. Other symbols (such as spaces or the ones above the number keys on your keyboard) are not allowed in variable names. The only catches are that

- The first character cannot be a number.
- The variable name cannot consist of only numbers.

>> **Length:** Most compilers these days allow you to have as many characters in the variable name as you want. Choose variable names long enough to make sense but short enough that you can type them easily. Most people prefer anywhere from five to ten characters or so.

Examples of acceptable variable names are `Count`, `current_name`, `address_1000`, and `LookupAmount`.

Manipulating Integer Variables

You can *manipulate* variables, which means that you can do arithmetic with their values. You can easily do the usual addition, subtraction, multiplication, and division. The characters that you use for the arithmetic operations are as follows:

Character	Arithmetic Operation
+	Addition
–	Subtraction
*	Multiplication
/	Division

You can, however, perform another operation with integers, and it has to do with remainders and division. The idea is that if you divide, for example, 16 by 3, the answer in whole numbers is *5 remainder 1.* This remainder is sometimes called a *modulus.*

REMEMBER

When working with integer variables, remember the two basic things you can do with variables: You can put a value into a variable, and you can retrieve a value from a variable. Therefore, when working with an integer variable, the idea is that you can retrieve its value, do some arithmetic on it, and then print the answer or store it back into the same variable or another variable.

Adding integer variables

If you want to add two integer variables, use the + symbol. You can either print the result or put it back into a variable.

The AddInteger example adds two variables (start and time) and then prints the answer to the console. The addition operation is shown in bold.

```
#include <iostream>

using namespace std;

int main()
{
    int start;
    int time;

    start = 37;
    time = 22;

    cout << start + time  << endl;
    return 0;
}
```

REMEMBER

This code starts with two integer variables called start and time. It then sets start to 37 and sets time to 22. Finally, it adds the two variables (to get 59) and prints the results. When you see start + time, + is the *operator* that tells what action to perform, and start and time are the *operands* upon which the operator acts.

You can also add numbers themselves to variables. The following line adds 5 to start and prints the result:

```
cout << start + 5 << endl;
```

Or you can save the value back in another variable, as in the following fragment:

```
total = start + 5;
cout << total << endl;
```

This example adds 5 to start and saves the new value in total.

WARNING

When you use code such as total = start + 5;, although you're adding 5 to start, you aren't actually changing the value stored in start. The start variable itself remains the same as it was before this statement runs. Instead, the computer figures out the result of start + 5 and saves that value inside total. Thus, total is the only variable that changes here.

This may seem strange at first, but you can actually do something like this:

```
total = total + 5;
```

This statement really just means you're going to add 5 to the value stored in total, and you'll take the value you get back and store it *back in total*. In other words, total will now be 5 greater than it was to begin with. The AddInteger3 example shows this technique in action:

```
#include <iostream>

using namespace std;

int main()
{
    int total;
    total = 12;
    cout << total << endl;

    total = total + 5;
    cout << total << endl;

    return 0;
}
```

When you run this application, you see the following output on the console:

```
12
17
```

C++ offers a shortcut for adding a value to a variable and storing it back in the variable. The line

```
total = total + 5;
```

is the same as

```
total += 5;
```

For this line, we would say, "Total plus equal five."

TIP

Think of the `total += 5` notation as simply a shortcut for `total = total + 5;`.

You can also use the `+=` notation with other variables. For example, if you want to add the value in `time` to the value in `total` and store the result back in `total`, you can do this:

```
total = total + time;
```

Or you can use this shortcut:

```
total += time;
```

If you're adding just 1 to a variable, which is called *incrementing the variable*, you can use an even shorter shortcut. It looks like this:

```
total++;
```

This is the same as `total = total + 1;` or `total += 1;`.

Subtracting integer variables

Everything you can do involving the addition of integer variables you can also do with subtraction. For example, you can subtract two variables, as shown in the `SubtractVariable` example:

```
#include <iostream>

using namespace std;

int main()
{
    int final;
    int time;

    final = 28;
    time = 18;

    cout << final - time << endl;
    return 0;
}
```

When this application runs, the console shows the number 10, which is 28 - 18. Remember that, as with addition, the value of neither final nor time actually changes. The computer just figures out the difference and prints the answer on the console without modifying either variable.

You can also subtract a number from a variable, and (as before) you still aren't changing the value of the variable, as in the following example:

```
cout << final - 5 << endl;
```

You can subtract one variable from another and save the result in a third variable:

```
start = final - time;
```

And you can change the value in a variable by using subtraction, as in the following line of code, which subtracts time from final and saves the result back in final:

```
final = final - time;
```

Or you can do the same thing by using the shortcut notation:

```
final -= time;
```

Finally, as with addition, you have a shortcut to a shortcut. If you want only to subtract 1, you can simply use two minus signs, as in the following:

```
Final--;
```

This line is pronounced *minus minus*. The -- is the *decrement operator*. When applied to a variable, it's called *decrementing the variable*.

Multiplying integer variables

To do multiplication in C++, you use the asterisk (*) symbol. As with addition and subtraction, you can multiply two variables, or you can multiply a variable by a number. You can either print the result or save it in a variable. For example, you can multiply two variables and print the results to the console with the following line:

```
cout << length * width << endl;
```

Or you can multiply a variable by a number, as in this line:

```
cout << length * 5 << endl;
```

And as with addition and subtraction, you can multiply two variables and save the result in a third variable:

```
area = length * width;
```

You can also use multiplication to modify a variable's value, as in

```
total = total * multiplier;
```

Or, to use the shortcut:

```
total *= multiplier;
```

And (as before) you can do the same with just a number:

```
total = total * 25;
```

Or this:

```
total *= 25;
```

Note that there is no ** operator used to multiply a value by 1 or by itself. Consequently, the compiler will raise an error if you type **total**;**.

Dividing integer variables

Although addition, subtraction, and multiplication are straightforward with integer variables, division is a bit trickier. The chief reason is that, with integer values, sometimes you just can't divide evenly.

In terms of strictly whole numbers, the answer to 21 divided by 5 is 4 *remainder* 1. And that's how the computer does arithmetic with integers. It gets two different answers: the *quotient* and the *remainder*. What's left over is the *remainder*.

Because two different answers to a division problem may occur, C++ uses two different operators for figuring these two different answers.

To find the quotient, use the slash (/). Think of this character as the usual division operator, because when you deal with integer values that divide evenly, this operator gives you the correct answer. Thus, 10 / 2 gives you 5, as you would expect. Most people just call this the division operator.

To find the remainder, use the percent sign (%). This is often called the *modulus operator*.

The DivideInteger example, shown next, takes two numbers and prints their quotient and remainder. Then it does it again for another pair of numbers. The first pair has no remainder, but the second pair does.

```cpp
#include <iostream>

using namespace std;

int main()
{
    int first, second;
    cout << "Dividing 28 by 14." << endl;
    first = 28;
    second = 14;
    cout << "Quotient   " << first / second
        << endl;
    cout << "Remainder " << first % second
        << endl;

    cout << "Dividing 32 by 6." << endl;
    first = 32;
    second = 6;
    cout << "Quotient   " << first / second
        << endl;
    cout << "Remainder " << first % second
        << endl;
    return 0;
}
```

When you run this application, you see the following output:

```
Dividing 28 by 14.
Quotient  2
Remainder 0
Dividing 32 by 6.
Quotient  5
Remainder 2
```

TIP

This code uses a couple new tricks in addition to the division tricks. You can combine the output of strings and numbers into a single cout statement. You did this for four of the cout statements. That's acceptable, as long as you string them together with the ‹‹ signs between each of them.

```
myRemainder = first % second;
```

TIP

The following shortcuts are available:

```
int first = 30;
int second = 33;
first /= 5;
second %= 5;
cout << first << " " second << endl;
```

Working with Character Variables

Another type of variable you can have is a character variable. A *character variable* can hold a single — *just one* — character that C++ stores as a number. It holds a value between –127 and 128 (char or signed char) or between 0 and 255 (unsigned char). Normally, a *character* is anything that can be typed, such as a letter of the alphabet, a digit, or another symbol you see on the computer keyboard, but a character can also hold nonprintable values found in an ASCII table (see https://en.cppreference.com/w/cpp/language/ascii). Some of these unprintable characters are *control characters* (so called because they control the appearance of text on the screen), such as the tab, carriage return, and newline character.

To declare a character variable, you use the type name char. To initialize a character variable, you put the character inside *single* quotes. The following is an example of a character:

```
char ch;
ch = 'a';
cout << ch << endl;
```

The character variable here is called ch, which is initialized to the character a. It's surrounded by single quotes. The code then prints it by using cout.

Null character

One important character in the programming world is the *null character*. The computer stores each character by using a number, and the null character's number is 0.

To notate the null character in C++, use \0, as in the following:

```
char mychar = '\0';
```

Nonprintable and other characters

The null character is an example of a *nonprintable character.* You can try to print one, but you get either a blank space or nothing at all, depending on the compiler.

But some characters are special in that they do something when you print, though you can't type them directly. One example is the newline character. The *newline character* (\n) symbolizes the start of a new line of text. In all cases, the computer places the *insertion point* (the place where it adds new characters) on the next line. If you're printing some text to the console and then you print a newline character, any text that follows will be on the next line.

The *carriage return* character (\r) places the insertion point at the start of the line, but not on a new line (which means that if you use just a carriage return on a computer expecting both a carriage return and a newline, you overwrite what's already on the line). That's true with pretty much every C++ compiler.

The tab character (\t) and other characters start with a backslash. These are individual characters, and you can have them inside a character variable, as in the following example, which prints the letter *a*, and then a tab, and then the letter *b*. Notice that, to get the tab character to go into the character variable, you have to use the backslash (\) and then a t:

```
char ch = '\t';
cout << "a" << ch << "b" << endl;
```

To put a double quote inside a string, you need to precede the double quote with a backslash so the computer won't think that the double quote is the end of the string. But because a character is surrounded by single quotes, you don't need to do this. You can just put a double quote inside the character, as in the following:

```
char ch = '"';
```

Of course, that raises an important question now: What about single quotes? This time, you *do* have to use the backslash:

```
char ch = '\'';
```

And finally, to put a backslash inside a character, you use two backslashes:

```
char ch = '\\';
```

When the compiler sees a backslash inside a string or a character, it treats the backslash as special and looks at whatever follows it. If you have something like ' \' with no other character inside the single quotes following it, the compiler thinks the final quote is to be combined with the backslash. And then it moves forward, expecting a single quote to follow, representing the end. Because a single quote doesn't appear, the compiler issues an error message.

Using Strings

A *string* is simply a set of characters strung together. The compiler knows the start and end of a string in your code based on the location of the double quotes.

You can create a variable that can hold a string. The type you use is string. The CreateString example, shown here, demonstrates how to use a string variable.

```
#include <iostream>

using namespace std;

int main()
{
    string mystring;
    mystring = "Hello there";
    cout << mystring << endl;
    return 0;
}
```

When you run this application, the string Hello there appears on the console. The first line inside main() creates a string variable called mystring. The second line initializes it to "Hello there". The third line prints the string to the console.

Getting a part of a string

Accessing the individual characters within a string is easy. Take a look at the following IndividualCharacter example:

```
#include <iostream>

using namespace std;

int main()
{
    string mystring;
    mystring = "abcdef";
    cout << mystring[2] << endl;
    return 0;
}
```

Notice that the ninth line, the cout line, has the word mystring followed by a 2 inside brackets ([2]). When you run this application, here's what you see:

```
c
```

That's it, just a letter c. The 2 inside brackets means that you want to access the *third* character of the string and only that character.

REMEMBER

C++ starts numbering the positions inside the string at 0. So for this string, mystring[0] is the first character, which happens to be a. Therefore, mystring[2] gets the *third* character. In general, this book uses *fourth position* to mean the fourth position, which you access through mystring[3]. (The number inside brackets is called an *index*.)

A string is made of characters. So, a single character within a string has the type char. This means that you can do something like this (as shown in the IndividualCharacter2 example):

```
#include <iostream>

using namespace std;

int main()
{
    string mystring;
    mystring = "abcdef";
    char mychar = mystring[2];
    cout << mychar << endl;
}
```

In this example, mychar is a variable of type char. The mystring[2] expression *evaluates* to a value of type char. So, the assignment is valid. When you run this, you once again see the single character in the third position:

```
c
```

Changing part of a string

Using the bracket notation, you can also change a character inside a string. The following code, for example, changes the second character in the string (that is, the one with index 1) from a b to a q:

```
string x = "abcdef";
x[1] = 'q';
cout << x << endl;
```

This code writes the string aqcdef to the console.

Adding onto a string

You can easily add to a string variable. The following lines of code use the += operator, which was also used in adding numbers:

```
string mystring;
mystring = "Hi ";
mystring += "there";
cout << mystring << endl;
```

The first line declares the string mystring. The second line initializes it to "Hi ". The third line uses the += operator, which appends something to the string — in this case, "there". So, after this line runs, the string called mystring contains the string "Hi there", and that's what appears on the console when the cout line runs. The programmer term for adding something to a string is *concatenation*.

You can also do something similar with characters. The following code snippet adds a single character to a string:

```
string mystring;
mystring = "abcdef";
mystring += 'g';
cout << mystring << endl;
```

This code creates a string with "abcdef" and then adds a 'g' character to the end to get "abcdefg". Then it writes the full "abcdefg" to the console.

Adding two strings

You can take two strings and add them together by using a plus sign (+), just as you can do with integers. The final result is a new string that has copies of the values of the two strings pushed together, side-by-side. For example, the following code adds first to second to get a new string called third:

```
string first = "hello ";
string second = "there";
string third = first + second;
cout << third << endl;
```

This code prints the value of `third`, which is `"hello there"`. (Notice that the string called `first` has a space at its end, which is inside quotes and, therefore, part of the string.) You can also add a *string constant* (that is, an actual string in your application surrounded by quotes) to an existing string variable, as shown here:

```
string first = "hello ";
string third = first + "there";
cout << third << endl;
```

You may be tempted to try to add two string constants together, like this:

```
string bigstring = "hello " + "there";
cout << bigstring << endl;
```

Unfortunately, this won't work. In C++, a string constant and a string are fundamentally different.

Telling the Truth with Boolean Variables

In addition to integers and strings, another type in C++ can be pretty useful: a *Boolean variable*. Whereas an integer variable is a storage bin that can hold any integer value, a Boolean variable can hold only one of two different values: a `true` or a `false`.

The type name for a Boolean variable is `bool`. Therefore, to declare a Boolean variable, you use a statement like this:

```
bool finished;
```

This line declares a Boolean variable called `finished`. Then you can put either a `true` or a `false` in this variable, as in the following:

```
finished = true;
```

Or:

```
finished = false;
```

When you print the value of a Boolean variable by using code like this:

```
cout << finished << endl;
```

You see either a 1 for true or a 0 for false. The reason is that the computer stores a 1 to represent true and a 0 to represent false.

Using Floating-Point Values in a Variable

You can declare and initialize a variable to hold a floating-point value like this:

```
float temperature = 98.7;
```

A float variable can have a floating-point value with a limited precision and magnitude:

>> **Precision:** The maximum number of *significant digits* (the digits that don't include leading and trailing zeros) that the value can have. Typically, it's around seven digits.

>> **Magnitude:** How small or how large the value can be. Typically, it's between 10^{-38} and 10^{+38}.

Therefore, you can set the values of float variables proton_mass (in kilograms) and grains_of_sand (on Earth):

```
float proton_mass =
    0.0000000000000000000000000001672622;
float grains_of_sand = 7500000000000000000;
```

You can use *scientific notation* where you include the *exponent* (a power of 10) to write very large or very small floating-point values. Write the positive or negative exponent after a small e or a capital E:

```
float proton_mass = 1.672622e-27;
float grains_of_sand = 7.5e+18;
```

A double variable can have a floating-point value with as many as around 15 significant digits and a magnitude typically between 10^{-308} and 10^{+308}. Therefore, you can write:

```
double sqrt2 = 1.4142135623731;
```

Printing Float and Double Values

By default, cout prints a few significant digits of a floating-point value, whether it's a float or a double, and it prints large or small floating-point values in scientific notation. But you can use the set_precision() function to tell cout how many digits to print after the decimal point, and the fixed flag to tell it not to use scientific notation, as demonstrated by the following example program, Floats.cpp:

```
#include <iostream>
#include <iomanip>

using namespace std;

int main()
{
    float temperature = 98.7;
    double sqrt2 = 1.4142135623731;

    float proton_mass =
        0.00000000000000000000000000001672622;
    float grains_of_sand = 7500000000000000000;

    cout << temperature << " " << sqrt2 << endl;
    cout << setprecision(12) << sqrt2 << endl;
    cout << setprecision(7) << proton_mass
        << " " << grains_of_sand << endl;
    cout << fixed << setprecision(30)
        << proton_mass << endl;
    cout << setprecision(0) << grains_of_sand
        << endl;

    cout << endl;

    cout << "The temperature is around"
```

```
   << setw(7) << temperature
   << " and sqrt2 is " << setw(5)
   << setprecision(2)
   << sqrt2 << " approximately." << endl;
}
```

The cout statements print the following lines:

```
98.7 1.41421
1.41421356237
1.672622e-27 7.5e+18
0.000000000000000000000000001673
7500000260257742848

The temperature is around      99 and sqrt2 is
  1.41 approximately.
```

By default, the first cout t printed at most 6 digits of temperature
and sqrt2 after the decimal points. Calling the function
setprecicsion(12) in the second cout told it to print 12 digits of
sqrt2 after the decimal point. Calling setprecicsion(7) in the
third cout told it to print the 7 digits of proton_mass after the
decimal point and two digits of grains_of_sand after the decimal point. Printing is in scientific notation by default. The fixed
flag in the fourth cout and setprecision(30) told cout to print
the very small value of proton_mass without using an exponent,
and cout also rounded the value to fit in the 30 digits. The fifth
cout (which remained fixed) and setprecision(0) printed the
very large value of grains_of_sand without a decimal fraction
and without an exponent. Use the flag scientific to reset cout
to use scientific notation.

Use the setw() function to specify how many print positions to
use. The printed value will be right-justified with leading blanks
if necessary. The last cout statement and its printed line demonstrate setw().

Floating-point values can print with erroneous digits if cout
tries to print too many digits, which you see in the last printed
line earlier. When cout printed the value of grains_of_sand as a
whole number, there were erroneous digits beyond the seven significant digits of a float value. You can try to minimize *round-off
errors* by using double instead of float.

To use `setprecision()`, `setw()`, `fixed`, and `scientific`, you must have

```
#include <iomanip>
```

They set properties of `cout`.

Making Your Code More Readable with Enumerations

Suppose you want to create a variable that holds the color `green`. Using the standard types of integers, floating-point numbers, characters, and letters, you don't have a lot of choices. You could just pick a number to represent each color and store that number in a variable. Or, you could have saved a string, as in `"green"`. But C++ presents a better alternative. It's called an *enumeration*, which mates a human-understandable name like `green` to a computer-friendly value like 2.

REMEMBER

For each type, there's a list of possible values. An integer, for example, can be a whole number within a particular range. Strings can be any characters, all strung together. But what if you want a value called `blue`? Or `red`? Or even `beige`? Then you need an *enumeration type.*

The following line creates an enumeration type:

```
enum CrayonColor {blue, red, green, yellow,
      black, beige};
```

You now have a new type called `CrayonColor`, which you can use the same way you can use other types, such as `int`, `double`, or `string`. For example, you can create variables of type `CrayonColor` and set the value of each one to one of the enumeration values in the curly braces:

```
CrayonColor line_color = black;
CrayonColor fill_color = blue;
```

The variable `line_color` is of type `CrayonColor`, and its value is `black`. The variable `fill_color` is also of type `CrayonColor`, and its value is `blue`.

Suppose you print the value of a `CrayonColor` variable, such as

```
cout << line_color;
```

You would see the value 4 printed. You can use enumeration values in your code, but C++ stores each value as an integer, and it's the integer value that's printed. In each enumeration type, C++ assigns 0 to the first enumeration value, 1 to the second value, 2 to the third value, and so on. Therefore, it assigns 4 to `black` for the enumeration `CrayonColor`.

TIP

If you work with `enums` (the code form of enumerations), you need to decide what to name your new type. For example, you can choose `CrayonColor` or `CrayonColors`. It's best to make the term singular, as in `CrayonColor`, because you use only one color at a time. When you declare a variable, it makes more sense: `CrayonColor fill_color;` would mean that `fill_color` is a *color* — not a group of *colors*.

Reading from the Console

Throughout this chapter and the preceding chapter, you see many examples of how to write information to the console. Writing to the console involves the use of `cout`, like this:

```
cout << "hi there" << endl;
```

Reading from the console (that is, getting a response from the user of your application, who is typing on the keyboard) uses the `cin` object (pronounced "see-in"). Next, instead of using the `<<` operator, you use the `>>` operator.

The `<<` operator is often called an *insertion operator* because you're writing to (or *inserting into*) a *stream,* which is nothing more than a bunch of characters going out somewhere. In the case of `cout`, those characters are going out to the console. The >> operator, on the other hand, is often called the *extraction operator*. The idea here is that you're extracting stuff from the stream. In the case of cin, you're extracting letters from the stream that the user is, in a sense, sending from the console into your application.

The ReadString example, shown here, demonstrates how you can read a string from the console:

```
#include <iostream>

using namespace std;

int main()
{
    string name;
    cout << "Type your name: ";
    cin >> name;
    cout << "Your name is " << name << endl;
    return 0;
}
```

When you run this code, you see the console ask you to type your name, and then it stops. That's because it's waiting for your input. Notice that the insertion point appears immediately after the text "Type your name:". That's because the first cout statement lacks the usual endl. It's normal to leave the insertion point, or cursor, on the same line as the question to avoid confusing the user. Type a name, such as Fred, without spaces and press Enter. The console then looks like this:

```
Type your name: Fred
Your name is Fred
```

The first line includes the name you typed, and the second line is whatever appears after you press Enter. Notice what happens: When you type a word and press Enter, the computer places that word in the name variable, which is a string. Then you can print name to the console by using cout.

You can also read integers, as in the following code (in the ReadInt example):

```cpp
#include <iostream>

using namespace std;

int main()
{
    int x;
    cout << "Type your favorite number: ";
    cin >> x;
    cout << "Your favorite number is " << x
         << endl;
    return 0;
}
```

This sample code reads a single integer into the variable x and then prints its value to the console.

REMEMBER

By default, cin reads words or numbers from the console separated by spaces. If you put spaces in your entry, only the first word gets read. cin reads the second word the next time the application encounters a cin >>.

IN THIS CHAPTER

» **Using comments**

» **Comparing numbers and evaluating other conditions**

» **Doing things based on a comparison**

» **Repeating code in specific ways**

» **Creating loops within loops**

Chapter **3**

Directing the Application Flow

This chapter considers different ways to evaluate conditions within your applications and cause different sections of code to run based on those conditions. It helps you understand how you can use C++ commands called *if statements*, which are similar to what-if situations in real life. You also see how to use other C++ statements (such as *do-while*) to perform *loops* (repeating the same application sections a number of times). But first we start by explaining comments.

Filling Your Code with Comments

A *comment* is simply some words in the code that the compiler ignores and that you include for the benefit of the humans reading the code. Comments are essential to good coding. You denote a comment in C++ by starting a line with two slashes, like this:

```
// Initialize total to the number
// of items involved.
```

```
total = 10;

// Now there are 3 more items.
total += 3;
```

Now anyone working on the project can understand what the code does. Note the blank line between the two groups of code. Using blank lines helps someone looking at the code see where one thought ends and another begins. The compiler ignores comments and blank lines; they're for the benefit of programmers reading the code. You can write whatever you want as comments, and the compiler pretends that the comments aren't even there.

TIP

A comment begins with //, and it can begin anywhere on the line. You can even put comments at the end of a line containing C++ code, instead of on a separate line. Using comments on a code line lets you focus a comment on just that line, like this:

```
int subtotal = 10;   // Initialize subtotal to 10.
```

This comment gives a little more explanation of what the line does. You usually use line comments like this when you want to tell others what kind of information a variable holds or explain a complex task. Normally, you explain blocks of code as shown earlier in this section.

TIP

You can use two kinds of comments in C++. One is the double slash (//). The other kind of comment begins with a slash-asterisk, /*, and ends with an asterisk-slash, */. The comments go between these delimiters and can span several lines, as in the following example:

```
/* This application separates the parts of the
   sandwich into its separate parts. This
   process is often called "separation of
   parts."
   (c) 2020 Sandwich Parts Separators, Inc.
*/
```

This is all one comment, and it spans multiple lines. You normally use this kind of comment to provide an overview of a task or describe the purpose of a function. This kind of comment also works well for the informational headings that some large company applications require. As with other comments, you can put them anywhere in your code, as long as you don't break a string or word in two by putting a comment in the middle.

Some beginning programmers get the mistaken idea that comments appear in the application window when the application runs. That isn't the case. A comment does not write anything to the console. To write things to the console, use cout (see Chapter 2).

Evaluating Conditions in C++

Most decisions that the computer makes are based on conditions evaluated by comparing either two numbers or two characters. For numerical comparisons, you may compare a variable to a number, as in the following statement:

```
x > 10
```

This comparison evaluates whether the variable x holds a value greater than the number 10. If x is, indeed, greater than 10, the computer sees this condition as true. If x is not greater than 10, the computer sees the condition as not true (false).

TIP

Developers often use the word *satisfied* with conditions. For the condition x > 10, if x is greater than 10, developers say the condition is satisfied.

For character comparisons, you may compare whether two characters are equal, as in the following statement:

```
mychar == 'A'
```

This comparison evaluates whether mychar contains the letter A. Notice that you use two equal signs, not just one. Using a single equal sign would assign the value A to mychar.

To test whether the character is not equal to something, you use the somewhat cryptic-looking != operator. Think of the ! as meaning *not*, as in:

```
mychar != 'X'
```

Finding the right C++ relational operators

Each statement in the previous section uses a *relational operator* to specify the comparison to make between the numbers or the strings. Table 3-1 shows you the types of relational operators available in C++ and the comparisons that they help you make in your applications.

TABLE 3-1 **Evaluating Numerical Conditions**

Operator	What It Means
<	Less than
<=	Less than or equal to
>	Greater than
>=	Greater than or equal to
==	Equal to
!=	Not equal to

The following list gives examples of the operators in action:

» The operator that tests for equality is *two* equal signs. It looks like this:

```
x == 10
```

When the computer finds this statement, it checks to see whether x equals 10.

WARNING

If you put just one equal sign in your statements, most C++ compilers will not give you an error message — though a statement like x = 10 is not really a condition! Instead, x = 10 is an *assignment,* setting the variable x to 10. When code contains such a statement, the result of the evaluation is always the same, regardless of the value of x.

REMEMBER

To test for all whole numbers greater than or equal to 10, the condition x > 9 works only if you're working with integers. If you're working with floating-point numbers, the statement x > 9 won't work the way you want. The number 9.1 is greater than 9, and it's not greater than or equal to 10. So if you want greater than or equal to and you're not working with integers, use the >= operator.

>> The operator that tests for inequality is an exclamation mark followed by an equal sign. For the condition x != 10, the condition evaluates as true only if x is not equal to 10 (x is equal to something other than 10).

>> When you're testing for greater-than or less-than conditions, the condition x > 10 is not true if the value of x is equal to 10. The condition x > 10 is true only if x is actually greater than, but not equal to, 10. To also test for x being equal to 10, you have two choices:

- If you're working with integers, you can test whether x > 9. In that case, the condition is true if x equals 10, or 11, or 12, and so on.

- You can use the greater-than-or-equal-to operator to determine equality: x >= 10. This condition also is true if x equals 10, 11, and so on.

To test for all whole numbers greater than or equal to 10, the condition x > 9 works only if you're working with integers. If you're working with floating-point numbers (see Chapter 2), the statement x > 9 won't work the way you want. The number 9.1 is greater than 9, and it's not greater than or equal to 10. So, if you want greater than or equal to and you're not working with integers, use the >= operator.

Combining multiple conditions

When you make evaluations for application decisions, you may have more than one condition to evaluate. You may have an expression with two conditions, and for the expression to be true, *either or both* conditions must be true. In other words, the expression is false only if *both* conditions are false. Combining conditions like this is an *or* expression: If this is true, or if that is true, or if both are true, then something happens.

To evaluate two conditions together in C++, you write them in the same expression and separate them with the *or* operator (||), which looks like two vertical bars, as shown in the following expression:

```
(i < 10) || (i > 100)
```

TIP

The optional parentheses help you to see the two conditions better. They aren't required by the expression.

In addition to an or condition, you can have an expression containing two conditions, and for the expression to be true, *both conditions* must be true. In other words, the expression is false if *either* condition is false. Combining conditions like this is an *and* expression: Only if both conditions are true, then something happens. An *and* expression in C++ uses the && operator, such as:

```
(i > 10) && (i < 100)
```

This expression checks to see whether a number is more than 10 *and* less than 100. The expression is true only if the number is in the range 11 through 99.

Combining conditions by using the && and || operators is a use of *logical operators*.

Using If Statements and Conditions

In C++, decisions usually take the form of an *if* statement, which is code that starts with the if keyword followed by a condition, which is often a numerical condition wherein two numbers are compared and then two blocks of code appear: one that runs if the condition is satisfied and one that runs if it is not.

Computers, like humans, evaluate conditions and use the results of the evaluations as input for making a decision. To decide on a plan of action based on a condition that your application evaluates, you use an *if* statement, which looks like this:

```
if (x > 10)
{
    cout << "Yuppers, it's greater than 10!"
        << endl;
}
```

This example translates into English as: If *x* is greater than 10, write the message

```
"Yuppers, it's greater than 10!"
```

In an *if* statement, the part inside the parentheses is called either the *test* or the *condition.* You usually apply *condition* to this part of the `if` statement and use the word *test* as a verb, as in "I will test whether *x* is greater than 10."

In C++, the condition for an *if* statement always goes inside parentheses. If you forget the parentheses, you'll get an error message.

Deciding what if and also what else

When you write code for a comparison, usually you want to tell the computer to do something if the condition is true and to do something else if the condition is not true. In the English language, you often see this kind of logic with the word *otherwise:* If such-and-such is true, I will do this; otherwise, I will do that.

In C++, you use the `else` keyword for the *otherwise* situation. The `IfElse` example demonstrates how to use the `else` keyword, as shown in the following code:

```cpp
#include <iostream>

using namespace std;

int main()
{
    int i;
    cout << "Type any number: ";
    cin >> i;

    if (i > 10)
    {
        cout << "It's greater than 10." << endl;
    }
    else
    {
        cout << "It's not greater than
10." << endl;
```

```
        }

        return 0;
}
```

In this code, you test whether a number is greater than 10. If it is, you print one message. If it is not, you print a different message. Notice how the two blocks of code are distinct. The first block immediately follows the *if* statement; it's the code that runs if the condition is `true`. The next block is preceded by the `else` keyword, and this block runs if the condition is `false`.

Going further with the else and if

The IfElse2 example shown in the following code demonstrates how to combine the `if` and `else` keywords to check for multiple alternatives:

```cpp
#include <iostream>

using namespace std;

int main()
{
    int i;
    cout << "Type any number: ";
    cin >> i;
    if (i > 10)
    {
        cout << "It's greater than 10." << endl;
    }
    else if (i == 10)
    {
        cout << "It's equal to 10" << endl;
    }
    else
    {
        cout << "It's less than 10." << endl;
    }
    return 0;
}
```

Making Decisions Using a Conditional Operator

Besides using an *if* statement, a C++ application can make decisions by using a *conditional operator*.

Think about this process: If two integer variables are equal, set a string variable to the string "equal". Otherwise, set it to the string "not equal". In other words, suppose that you have two integer variables, called first and second. first has the value 10 in it, and second has the value 20 in it. You also have a string variable called result. Now, to follow the little process just described: Are the two variables equal? No, they are not, so you set result to the string "not equal".

Now do this in C++. First, you declare the variables first, second, and result:

```
int first = 10;
int second = 20;
string result;
```

Notice that you didn't yet initialize the string variable result. But now you're going to write a single line of code that performs the process just described:

```
result = (first == second) ? "equal" :
    "not equal";
```

In English, this means result gets "equal" if first is equal to second; otherwise, it gets "not equal".

The colon separates two results, one of which will be assigned to the result variable. If first is equal to second, result gets the string "equal". Otherwise, it gets the string "not equal".

Remember that the variable on the left side of the single equal sign receives the value of the expression on the right side of the equal sign, which evaluates to be a string of either "equal" or

"not equal", depending on the result of the condition. The whole
EqualityCheck example is shown here:

```
#include <iostream>

using namespace std;

int main()
{
    int first = 10;
    int second = 20;
    string result;

    result = first == second ? "equal" :
        "not equal";

    cout << result << endl;
    return 0;
}
```

BOOLEAN VARIABLES AND CONDITIONAL OPERATORS

You can use Boolean variables with conditional operators. In a conditional operator such as

```
result = (first == second) ? "equal" : "not equal";
```

the condition (first == second) actually works out to be a
Boolean value — either true or false. Therefore, you can rewrite
part of the previous example:

```
string result;

bool isequal;

isequal = (first == second);

result = isequal ? "equal" : "not equal";
```

Repeating Actions with Statements That Loop

Applications often have loops.

Table 3-2 shows the types of loops. As the chapter progresses, you see examples of using all three loop types.

TABLE 3-2 Choosing Your Loops

Type of Loop	Appearance
for	`for (x=0; x<10; x++) { }`
while	`while (x < 10) { }`
do-while	`do { } while (x < 10)`

You may want to use these loops in the following situations:

>> *for* **loop:** Use a *for* loop when you have a counter variable and you want it to loop while the counter variable increases or decreases over a range. The *for* loop is a good choice if you know how many times you want the loop to execute.

>> *while* **loop:** Use the *while* loop when you have a condition under which you want your loop code to run. It's a good choice when you want to perform the test at the beginning of the loop. The test may fail immediately, so the loop may not execute even once.

>> *do-while* **loop:** Use the *do-while* loop when you have a condition under which you want your loop code to run and you want to ensure that the loop always runs at least once, even if the condition isn't satisfied. It's a good choice when the code inside the loop prepares the variables that the test uses, so the loop must execute at least once.

Looping for

Using the *for* loop provides precise control over how many times the code performs a task. In addition, it's extremely flexible because you also have control over how the counter variable updates.

Performing a simple for loop

To use a *for* loop, you use the for keyword and follow it with a set of parentheses that contains information regarding the number of times the *for* loop executes.

For example, when adding the numbers from 1 to 100, you want a variable that starts with the number 1; then you add 1 to x, increase the variable to 2, and add the next number to x again over and over. The common action here that doesn't change each time is the "add it to x" part, and the part that changes is the variable, called a *control variable.* Your application executes a block of code each time through the loop using the current value of the control variable.

The control variable, therefore, starts at 1 and goes through 100. Does it include 100? Yes. And with each iteration, you add 1 to the control variable. The *for* statement looks like this:

```
for (i = 1; i <= 100; i++)
```

This statement means that the control variable, i, starts at 1, and the loop runs over and over while i is less than or equal to 100. After each iteration, the control variable increments by 1 because of the i++ statement.

Here are the three portions inside the parentheses of the *for* loop:

>> **Initializer:** You use this first portion to set up the control variable.

>> **Condition:** It's the condition under which the loop continues to run.

>> **Finalizer:** In this third portion, you specify what happens after each cycle of the loop.

WARNING

Three items are inside the *for* loop, and you separate them with semicolons. If you try to use commas, your code won't compile.

To tell the computer the work to do with each iteration, follow the *for* statement with a set of braces containing the statements you want to execute with each iteration. So, to add the value of the control variable to x, you would do this:

```
for (i = 1; i <=100; i++)
{
```

```
        x += i;
}
```

Note that if the for loop only executes one statement, you don't
have to include the braces. This example would add i to x with
each loop. Of course, you must create x and assign an initial value
to it to make the loop work. The ForLoop example demonstrates
the *for* loop in its final form, complete with the way to write the
final value of x to the console after the loop is finished:

```cpp
#include <iostream>

using namespace std;

int main()
{
    int x = 0;
    int i;

    for (i = 1; i <= 100; i++)
    {
        x += i;
    }

    cout << x << endl;
    return 0;
}
```

When you run this example, you see an output of 5050. Notice a
few things about this block of code.

>> You declare both variables that you're working with: x and i.

>> The *for* statement initializes the control variable, specifies the
condition under which it continues running, and tells what to
do after each iteration. In this example, the *for* loop starts with
i = 1, and it runs as long as i is less than or equal to 100.
For each iteration, the computer adds the value of i to x; the
process that adds the value to x is the code inside the braces.

>> The computer adds 1 to i, which you specify as the third item
inside the parentheses. The computer does this part, adding 1
to i, only after it finishes executing the stuff inside the braces.

The final portion of the *for* statement must be a complete state-ment in itself. If the statement fails to update the control variable and the condition never becomes false, your *for* loop can run for-ever until you force your program to terminate. This programming error is known as an *infinite loop.*

Going backward

If you need to count backward, you can do that with a *for* loop as well. To count backward, you set up the three portions of the *for* loop: the initial setup, the condition under which it continues to run, and the action after each iteration.

For the first portion, you set the control variable to the starting value, the top number. For the condition, you check whether the control variable's value continues to be greater than or equal to the final number. And for the third portion, you *decrement* the counter (reduce its value by 1) rather than increment it. Thus, you would have the following:

```
for (i=10; i>=5; i--)
```

This line starts the control variable i at 10. The *for* loop decre-ments i by 1 after each iteration, so the value of i becomes 9, then 8, then 7, and so on. This process continues as long as i is at least 5. So, i counts 10, 9, 8, 7, 6, 5. The whole application may look like the ForCountdown example, shown here:

```
#include <iostream>

using namespace std;

int main()
{
    for (int i=10; i>=5; i--)
    {
        cout << i << endl;
    }

    return 0;
}
```

When you run this code, you see the following output:

```
10
9
8
7
6
5
```

Looping while

Often, you find that *for* loops work only so well. Sometimes, you don't want a control variable; you just want to run a loop over and over as long as a certain situation is true. Then, after that situation is no longer the case, you want to stop the loop.

To do this in C++, you use a *while* statement. The while keyword is followed by a set of parentheses containing the condition under which the application is to continue running the loop. Whereas the general *for* statement's parentheses include three portions that show how to change the counter variable, the *while* statement's parentheses contain only a condition. The WhileLoop example demonstrates a simple *while* loop, as shown here:

```cpp
#include <iostream>

using namespace std;

int main()
{
    int i = 0;
    while (i <= 5)
    {
        cout << i << endl;
        i++;
    }
    cout << "All Finished!" << endl;
    return 0;
}
```

This code runs while i is less than or equal to 5. Thus, the output of this application is:

```
0
1
2
3
4
5
All Finished!
```

REMEMBER

Notice that you must declare i outside the *while* loop using int i = 0;.

The *while* loop is handy if you don't have a particular number of times you need the loop to run.

Often, for this kind of situation, you create a Boolean variable called done and start it out as false. The *while* statement is simply:

```
while (!done)
```

This line translates easily to English as "While not done, do the following." Then, inside the *while* loop, when the situation happens that you know the loop must finish, you set the following:

```
done = true;
```

The WhileLoop2 example demonstrates how to do this sort of process:

```cpp
#include <iostream>

using namespace std;

int main()
{
    int i = 0;
    bool done = false;
    while (!done)
    {
        cout << i << endl;
```

```
        i++;
        if (i > 5)
            done = true;
    }
    cout << "All Finished!" << endl;
    return 0;
}
```

The variable used to control the loop condition (here, it's variable done) must change, or the loop will continue to run forever.

Doing while

The *while* statement has a cousin in the family: the *do-while* statement. A loop of this form is similar to the *while* loop, but with an interesting little catch: The *while* statement goes at the end, which means the loop always executes at least one time. The DoWhileLoop example demonstrates how to use this kind of loop:

```
#include <iostream>

using namespace std;

int main()
{
    int i = 15;
    do
    {
        cout << i << endl;
        i++;
    }
    while (i <= 5);
    cout << "All Finished!" << endl;
    return 0;
}
```

Notice here that the loop starts with the do keyword; then the material for the loop follows inside braces; and finally the *while* statement appears at the end. Because the condition is evaluated at the end of the loop, the loop executes at least once. Therefore, the output from this example is a little different from the other *while* loop examples:

```
15
All Finished!
```

Breaking and Continuing

Sometimes, you may write an application that includes a loop that does more than simply add numbers. You may find that you want the loop to end under a condition that's separate from the condition in the loop declaration. Or you may want the loop to suddenly skip out of the current loop and continue with the next item in the loop when the item being processed is incorrect in some way. When you stop a loop and continue with the code after the loop, you use a *break* statement. When you quit the current cycle of the loop and continue with the next cycle, you use a *continue* statement. The next two sections show you how to do this.

REMEMBER

Even though the examples in the following sections rely on a *for* loop, the *break* and *continue* statements also work for *while* and *do-while* loops.

Breaking

Suppose you're writing an application that reads data over the internet, and the loop runs for the amount of data that's supposed to come. But midway through the process, you encounter some data that has an error in it, and you want to get out of the *for* loop immediately.

C++ includes a handy little statement that can rescue you in such a situation. The statement is called *break*. It breaks you out of the loop.

The ForLoop3 example that follows demonstrates this technique. This sample checks for the special case of i equaling 5. You could accomplish the same result by changing the end condition of the *for* loop, but at least it shows you how the *break* statement works.

```
#include <iostream>

using namespace std;

int main()
{
    for (int i=0; i<10; i++)
    {
        cout << i << " ";
        if (i == 5)
        {
            break;
        }
        cout << i * 2 << endl;
    }
    cout << "All Finished!" << endl;
    return 0;
}
```

In the preceding code, the first line inside the *for* loop, cout << i
<< " ";, runs when i is 5. But the final line in the *for* loop, cout
<< i * 2 << endl;, does not run when i is 5 because you tell it to
break out of the loop between the two cout statements.

Also notice that when you break out of the loop, the application
doesn't quit. It continues with the statements that follow the
loop. In this case, it still prints the message "All Finished!".

Continuing

In addition to the times when you may need to break out of a loop
for a special situation, you can also cause the loop to end its current iteration; but instead of breaking out of it, the loop resumes
with the next iteration.

To do this trick, you use a C++ statement called *continue*. The
continue statement says, "End the current iteration, but continue
running the loop with the next iteration."

The ForLoop4 example that follows shows a slightly modified version of the previous example, in the "Breaking" section. When the
loop gets to 5, it doesn't execute the second cout line. But rather

than break out of the loop, it continues with 6, and then 7, and so on until the loop finishes on its own:

```cpp
#include <iostream>

using namespace std;

int main()
{
    int i;
    for (i=0; i<10; i++)
    {
        cout << i << " ";
        if (i == 5)
        {
            cout << endl;
            continue;
        }
        cout << i * 2 << endl;
    }
    cout << "All Finished!" << endl;
    return 0;
}
```

Nesting Loops

A *nested loop* is simply a loop inside a loop. Suppose you want to multiply each of the numbers 1 through 10 by 1 and print the answer for each multiplication, and then you want to multiply each of the numbers 1 through 10 by 2 and print the answer for each multiplication, and so on, up to a multiplier of 10. Your C++ code would look like the ForLoop5 example:

```cpp
#include <iostream>

using namespace std;

int main()
{
    for (int x = 1; x <= 10; x++)
```

```
{
    cout << "Products of " << x <<endl;
    for (int y = 1; y <= 10; y++)
    {
        cout << x * y << endl;
    }
    cout << endl;
}
return 0;
}
```

In this example, you have a loop inside a loop. The inner loop can make use of x from the outer loop. Yes, you can have a loop inside a loop inside a loop inside a loop. You can also place any loop inside any other loop, like a *while* loop inside a *for* loop.

Notice you have a cout call before and after the inner loop. You can do this; your inner loop doesn't have to be the only statements inside the outer loop.

WARNING

Although you can certainly have a loop inside a loop inside a loop inside a loop, the deeper you get, the more potentially confusing your code can become, so try not to get carried away with nesting.

Using Switch Statements

Many times in programming, you may want to compare a variable to one thing, and if it doesn't match, compare it to another and another and another. To do this with an *if* statement, you need to use a whole bunch of else if lines. Using *if* statements works out pretty well, but you can do it in another way: Use the *switch* statement.

WARNING

The approach shown in this section doesn't work for all types of variables. In fact, it works with integers, characters, and enumerations. It won't even work with character strings. However, when you need to make multiple comparisons for integers and characters, using this approach is quite useful.

Here's a complete *switch* statement that you can refer to as you read about the individual parts in the paragraphs that follow.

This *switch* statement compares x to 1, and then 2, and, finally, includes a catchall section called default if x is neither 1 nor 2:

```
int x;
cin >> x;
switch (x)
{
    case 1:
        cout << "It's 1!" << endl;
        break;
    case 2:
        cout << "It's 2!" << endl;
        break;
    default:
        cout << "It's something else!" << endl;
        break;
}
```

To use the *switch* statement, you type the word **switch** and then the variable or expression that you want to test in parentheses. Suppose that x is type int and you want to compare it to several different values. You would first type:

```
switch (x) {
```

The preceding item in parentheses isn't a comparison; it's a variable. You can also put complex expressions inside the parentheses, but they must evaluate to either an integer or a character. For example, if x is an integer, you can test the following because x + 5 is still an integer:

```
switch (x + 5) {
```

REMEMBER

A *switch* statement compares only a single variable or expression against several different items. If you have complex comparisons, you instead use a compound *if* statement.

After the header line for the *switch* statement, you list the values you want to compare the expression to. Each entry starts with the word case followed by the value to compare the expression against, and then a colon, as in the following:

```
case 1:
```

Next is the code to run in the event that the expression matches this case (here, 1):

```
cout << "It's 1" << endl;
```

To complete a specific case, you add the word break. Every case in the switch statement usually has a break line, which ends the case. If you leave out the break statement (either purposely or accidentally), when the computer runs this case, execution continues with the next case statement code. This is a second purpose of the *break* statement. You saw it used earlier to break out of loops.

Note that the end of the example switch block has a final default case. It applies to the situation when none of the preceding cases applies. The default case isn't required; you can leave it off if you don't need it. However, if you do include it, you put it at the end of the switch block because it's the catchall case.

The following SwitchStatement example is a complete application that demonstrates a *switch* statement. It also shows you how you can make a simple, antiquated-looking menu application on the console. You don't need to press Enter after you choose the menu item; you just press the key for your menu selection. That's thanks to the use of getch() rather than cin. The comments help explain the program's logic.

```
#include <iostream>
#include <conio.h>

using namespace std;

int main() {
    // Display a list of options.
    cout << "Choose your favorite:" << endl;
    cout << "1. Apples " << endl;
    cout << "2. Bananas " << endl;
    cout << "3. Lobster " << endl;

    // Obtain the user's selection.
    char ch = getch();

    // Continue getting user selections until the
    // user enters a valid number.
```

```cpp
    while (ch < '1' || ch > '3') {
      ch = getch();
    }

    // Use a switch to display the user's
    // selection.
    cout << "You chose " << ch << endl;
    switch (ch) {
    case '1':
      cout << "Apples are good for you!" << endl;
      break;
    case '2':
      cout << "Bananas have plenty of potassium!"
           << endl;
      break;
    case '3':
      cout << "Expensive, but you have good taste!"
           << endl;
      break;
    }

    return 0;
}
```

Chapter **4**

Dividing Your Work with Functions

People generally agree that most projects throughout life are easier when you divide them into smaller, more manageable tasks. That's also the case with computer programming — if you break your code into smaller pieces, it becomes more manageable.

C++ provides many ways to divide code into smaller portions. One way is through the use of functions. A *function* is a set of lines of code that performs a particular job. In this chapter, you discover what functions are and how you can use them to make your programming job easier.

Dividing Your Work

When you write a computer application, after you divide your job into smaller pieces called *objects*, you eventually start giving these objects behaviors. And to code these behaviors, you break them into manageable parts called *functions*. Think of a function as a machine. You can put one or more values into the machine; it processes them, and then it spits out a single answer, if anything at all.

This machine (or function) has three main parts:

>> **Inputs:** The function can receive data through its inputs. These data elements can be numbers, strings, or any other type. When you create such a machine, you can have as many inputs as you want (or even none).

>> **Processor:** The processor is the function itself. In terms of C++, this is actually a set of code lines.

>> **Output:** A function can *return* something when it has finished doing its thing. In C++, this output is in the form of numbers, strings, or any other type.

To make all this clear, try out the following FirstFunction code. (Don't forget the second line, #include<math.h>, which gives you some math capabilities.)

```
#include <iostream>
#include <math.h>

using namespace std;

int main()
{
    cout << fabs(-10.5) << endl;
    cout << fabs(10.5) << endl;
    return 0;
}
```

When you run this application, you see the following output:

```
10.5
10.5
```

In this code, you use a function or machine called fabs(). This function takes a number as input and returns as output the absolute value of the number.

REMEMBER

The reason for the f before the name abs is that it uses floating-point numbers, which are simply numbers with decimal points.

So, the first line inside main( ) *calls* fabs( ) for the value –10.5. The cout then takes the output of this function (that is, the *result*) and prints it to the console.

Then the second line does the same thing again, except that it takes the absolute value of the number 10.5.

And where is the processor for this function? It's not in your code; it's in another file, and the following line ensures that your application can use this function:

```
#include <math.h>
```

You've seen functions in many places. If you use a calculator and enter a number and press the square root button, the calculator runs a function that calculates the square root.

Calling a Function

When you run the code in a function, you're *calling* the function. When you call a function, you do so by name.

To call a function, you type its name and then a set of parentheses. Inside the parentheses, you list the items you want to send to the inputs of the function. The term used here is *pass*, as in "You pass the values to the function."

For example, if you want to call the fabs( ) function, you type **fabs**, an open parenthesis, the number you want to pass to it, and then a closed parenthesis, as in the following example:

```
fabs(-10.5)
```

The fabs( ) function returns a value — the absolute value of –10.5, and you probably want to do something with that value. You could, for example, print it to the console:

```
cout << fabs(-10.5) << endl;
```

Or you could store it away in another variable. Before you can do that, you need to know the *type* that the function returns. Just as with a variable, a function return value has a type. In this case, the type is double. To save the result of fabs(), you need to have a variable of type double. The following Fabs2 example does this:

```
#include <iostream>
#include <math.h>

using namespace std;

int main()
{
  double mynumber = fabs(-23.87);
  cout << mynumber << endl;
  return 0;
}
```

This code declares a double variable called mynumber. Then it calls fabs(), passing it -23.87 and returning the value into mynumber. Next, it prints the value in mynumber to the console.

When you run this application, you see the following, which is the absolute value of -23.87:

```
23.87
```

Passing a variable

You can also pass the value of a variable into a function. The following Fabs3 example creates two variables: One is passed into the function, and the other receives the result of the function.

```
#include <iostream>
#include <math.h>

using namespace std;

int main()
{
  double start = -253.895;
  double finish = fabs(start);
  cout << finish << endl;
  return 0;
}
```

This code creates two variables; the first is called start, and the second is called finish. It initializes start with a value of –253.895. Next, it calls fabs(), passing it the value of start. It saves the return value in finish, and prints the value in finish. When Fabs3 runs, you see the following appear on the console:

```
253.895
```

TIP

Saving a function result to a variable is useful if you need to use the result several times over.

Passing multiple variables

Some functions have multiple parameters. As with functions that take a single value, you put the values inside a single set of parentheses. Because you have multiple values, you separate them with commas. The following Pow1 example uses a function called pow() to calculate the third power of 10. Make sure that you include the math.h line in the include section so that you can use the pow() function.

```cpp
#include <iostream>
#include <math.h>

using namespace std;

int main()
{
    double number = 10.0;
    double exponent = 3.0;
    cout << pow(number, exponent) << endl;
    return 0;
}
```

When you run the application, you see 10 to the third power, which is 1,000:

```
1000
```

You can also pass a mixture of variables and numbers in expressions, or just numbers. The following code snippet also calculates the third power of 10 but passes an actual number, 3.0, for the power:

```
double number = 10.0;
cout << pow(number, 3.0) << endl;
```

Or you can pass only numbers:

```
cout << pow(10.0, 3.0) << endl;
```

Writing Your Own Functions

Calling functions is great, but you get real power when you write your own, specialized functions. Before writing a function, remember the parts: the inputs, the main code or processor, and the single output (or no output). The inputs, however, are called *parameters,* and the output is called a *return value.*

The following AddOne example provides both a custom function and code in main() that calls the custom function. (The function is placed outside main() — before it, in fact.)

```
#include <iostream>

using namespace std;

int AddOne(int start)
{
   int newnumber = start + 1;
   return newnumber;
}

int main()
{
   int testnumber = 20;
   int result = AddOne(testnumber);
   cout << result << endl;
   return 0;
}
```

REMEMBER

Notice that this example lacks the #include <math.h> entry found in earlier examples. You need to add an entry to the include section of your code only when you use a feature of that include file. In this case, the example relies on standard math features that are part of the basic C++ language, so you don't need any additional code.

After you run the example, you see:

```
21
```

TIP

When you write your own functions, try to choose a name that makes sense and describes what the function does.

Improving On the Basic Function

Not all functions work precisely the same way. You can create functions that have multiple parameters or no parameters. There is no law that says that a function must absolutely provide a return value. The following sections discuss variations on the basic function theme discussed in the previous section.

Using multiple parameters or no parameters

You don't need to write your functions with only one parameter each. You can have several parameters, or you can have none. Here are some ideas for functions:

>> **Day:** Determines the day and returns it as a string, as in "Monday" or "Tuesday"

>> **Number-of-users:** Figures out the current number of users logged in to a web-server computer

>> **Current font:** In a text editor application (such as Notepad), returns a string containing the current font name, such as "Arial"

>> **Editing time:** Returns the amount of time you've been using the word processor application

>> **Username:** If you're logged on to a computer, gives back your username as a string, such as "Elisha"

All functions in this list have something in common: They look up information.

If a function takes no parameters, you write the function header as you would for one that takes parameters, and you include the parentheses; you just don't put anything *in* the parentheses, as the following UserName example shows:

```
#include <iostream>

using namespace std;

string Username()
{
  return "Elisha";
}

int main()
{
  cout << Username() << endl;
  return 0;
}
```

When you run this code, you see the following output:

```
Elisha
```

Your function can also take multiple parameters. The following ConnectNames example demonstrates the use of multiple parameters. Notice that the function, ConnectNames(), takes the two strings as parameters and combines them, along with a space in the middle. Notice also that the function uses the two strings as variables.

```
#include <iostream>

using namespace std;

string ConnectNames(string first, string last)
{
  return first + " " + last;
}

int main()
```

```
{
    cout << ConnectNames("Richard", "Nixon")
        << endl;
    return 0;
}
```

In the function header, you see the type name `string` for each parameter. Each parameter requires its own type entry or the compiler displays an error. Here are some points about this code:

>> **You didn't create variables for the two names in** `main()`.
Instead, you just typed them as string constants (that is, as actual strings surrounded by quotes).

>> **You can do calculations and figuring right inside the**
`return` **statement.** That saves the extra work of creating a variable. In the function, you could create a return variable of type `string`, set it to `first + " " + last`, and then return that variable, as in the following code:

```
string result = first + " " + last;

return result;
```

But instead, the example shows how to do it all on one line, as in this line:

```
return first + " " + last;
```

Returning nothing

Look at the case in which a function doesn't return anything. In C++, the way you state that the function doesn't return anything is by using the keyword `void` as the return type in the function header. The following `SetUserName` example demonstrates this approach.

```
#include <iostream>

using namespace std;

void SetUsername(string newname)
{
```

```
   cout << "New user is " << newname << endl;
}

int main()
{
   SetUsername("Harold");
   return 0;
}
```

When you run the application, you see

```
New user is Harold
```

Notice the SetUsername() function header: It starts with the word void, which means that it returns nothing at all.

Don't try to return something in a function that has a return type of void. *Void* means that the function returns nothing at all. If you try to put a *return* statement in your function, you get a compile error.

Keeping your variables local

When you create a variable inside the code for a function, that variable will be known only to that particular function. When you create such variables, they're called *local variables,* and people say that they're "local" to that particular function.

To see a local variable at work, consider the code in the PrintName example:

```
#include <iostream>

using namespace std;

void PrintName(string first, string last)
{
   string fullname = first + " " + last;
   cout << fullname << endl;
}

int main()
{
```

```
   PrintName("Thomas", "Jefferson");
   return 0;
}
```

Notice in the `PrintName()` function that you declare a variable called `fullname`. You then use that variable in the second line in that function, the one starting with `cout`. But you can't use the variable inside `main()`. If you try to, as in the following code, you get a compile error:

```
int main()
{
   PrintName("Thomas", "Jefferson");
   cout << fullname << endl;
   return 0;
}
```

However, you can *declare* a variable called `fullname` inside `main()`, as in the `PrintName2` example. But, if you do that, this `fullname` is local only to `main()`, whereas the other variable, also called `fullname`, is local only to the `PrintName()` function. In other words, each function has its own variable; they just happen to share the same name. But they are *two separate variables*:

```
#include <iostream>

using namespace std;

void PrintName(string first, string last)
{
   string fullname = first + " " + last;
   cout << fullname << endl;
}

int main()
{
   string fullname = "Abraham Lincoln";
   PrintName("Thomas", "Jefferson");
   cout << fullname << endl;
   return 0;
}
```

When two functions declare variables by the same name, they're two separate variables. If you store a value inside one of them, the other function doesn't know about it. The other function only knows about its own variable by that name. As a result, the output from this example is:

```
Thomas Jefferson
Abraham Lincoln
```

If you use the same variable name in two different functions, forgetting that you're working with two different variables is very easy. Do this only if you're sure that no confusion can occur.

If you use the same variable name in two different functions (such as a control variable called index, which you use in a *for* loop), matching the case is usually a good idea. Don't use count in one function and use Count in another. Although you can certainly do that, you may find yourself typing the name wrong when you need it. But that won't cause you to access the other one. (You can't, because it's in a different function.) Instead, you get an error message, and you have to go back and fix it. Being consistent is a time-saver.

Forward references and function prototypes

All examples in this chapter place the function code above the code for main(). The reason is that the compiler scans the code from start to finish. If it hasn't yet encountered a function but sees a call to it, it doesn't know what it's seeing, and it issues an error message.

You can, however, place your functions after main(); or you can even use function prototypes to put your functions in other source code files.

A *function prototype* is nothing more than a copy of the function header. But rather than follow it with an open brace and then the code for the function, you follow the function header with a semicolon and you're finished. A function prototype looks like this:

```
void PrintName(string first, string last);
```

Then you actually write the full function (header, code, and all) later. The full function can even be later than main() or later than any place that makes calls to it.

Notice that this example looks just like the first line of a function. To write it, you simply copy the first line of the original function you write and add a semicolon. The following PrintName3 example shows how to use this technique:

```cpp
#include <iostream>

using namespace std;

void PrintName(string first, string last);

int main()
{
  PrintName("Thomas", "Jefferson");
  return 0;
}

void PrintName(string first, string last)
{
  string fullname = first + " " + last;
  cout << fullname << endl;
}
```

Notice that the function header appears above main() and ends with a semicolon. Next comes main(). Finally, you see the PrintName() function itself (again, with the header but no semicolon this time). Thus, the function comes after main().

If you have a source code file with, say, 20 functions, and these functions all make various calls to each other, it could be difficult to carefully order them so that each function calls *only* functions that are above it in the source code file. Instead, most programmers put the functions in some logical order, and they don't worry much about the calling order. Then they have all the function prototypes toward the top of the source code file, as shown in the last code block.

When you type a function prototype, many people say that you're specifying a *forward reference*. This term simply means that you're providing a reference to something that happens later.

Writing two versions of the same function

Sometimes you may want to write two versions of the same function, with the only difference being that they take different parameter types. For example, you may want a function called Combine(). One version takes two strings and puts the two strings together, but with a space in the middle. It then prints the resulting string to the console. Another version adds two numbers and writes all three numbers — the first two and the sum — to the console. The first version would look like this:

```
void Combine(string first, string second)
{
  cout << first << " " << second << endl;
}
```

The code for the function prints the two strings with a space between them. Now the second version looks like this:

```
void Combine(int first, int second)
{
  int sum = first + second;
  cout << first << " " << second << " " << sum
      << endl;
}
```

The function name is Combine(), and it doesn't return anything. But this version takes two integers, not two strings, as parameters. The code is also different from the previous code in that it first computes the sum of the inputs and then prints the different numbers.

REMEMBER

Overloading (using one name for multiple functions) is somewhat common in C++. The following Combine example contains the entire code. Both functions are present in the code.

```
#include <iostream>

using namespace std;

void Combine(string first, string second)
```

```
{
  cout << first << " " << second << endl;
}

void Combine(int first, int second)
{
  int sum = first + second;
  cout << first << " " << second << " "
      << sum << endl;
}

int main()
{
  Combine("David","Letterman");
  Combine(15,20);
  return 0;
}
```

You see each function called in main(). The compiler chooses which function to call based on the arguments you provide. For example, when viewing this call, you see two strings:

```
Combine("David","Letterman");
```

The compiler knows to use the first version, which takes two strings. Now look at the second function call:

```
Combine(15,20);
```

This call takes two integers, so the compiler knows to use the second version of the function.

When you overload a function, the parameters must differ (or must appear in a different order). For example, the functions can take the same type of information but use a different number of parameters. Of course, the previous example shows that the parameters can also vary by type. You can also have different return types, though they must differ by more than just the return type, and varying the parameter names doesn't count. The compiler will see Combine(string A, string B) and Combine(string First, string Second) as the same function.

Calling All String Functions

To get the most out of strings, you need to make use of some special functions that cater to the strings. However, using these functions is a little different from the other functions used so far in this chapter. Instead of just calling the function, you first type the variable name that holds the string, and then a period (or *dot*), and then the function name along with any arguments.

Inserting a string into a string

One function that you can use is `insert()`. You can use this function if you want to insert more characters into another string. For example, if you have the string `"Something interesting and bizarre"` and you insert the string `"seriously "` (with a space at the end) into the middle of it starting at index 10, you get the string `"Something seriously interesting and bizarre"`.

REMEMBER

When you work with strings, the first character is the 0th index, the second character is the 1st index, and so on. The following lines of code perform an insert by using the `insert()` function at index 10, even though you perform the insertion at letter 11:

```
string words = "Something interesting and
    bizarre";
words.insert(10, "seriously ");
```

The first of these lines simply creates a string called words and stuffs it full with the phrase `"Something interesting and bizarre"`. The second line does the insert. Notice the strange way of calling the function: You first specify the variable name, words, and then a dot, and then the function name, insert. Next, you follow it with the parameters in parentheses, as usual. For this function, the first parameter is the index where you want to insert the string. The second parameter is the actual string you're going to insert. After these two lines run, the string variable called words contains the string `"Something seriously interesting and bizarre"`.

Removing parts of a string

You can also erase parts of a string by using a similar function called `erase()`. The following line of code erases 16 characters from the words string starting at index 19:

```
words.erase(19,16);
```

Consequently, if the variable called words contains the string "Something seriously interesting and bizarre", after this line runs, it will contain "Something seriously bizarre".

Replacing parts of a string

Another useful function is replace(). This function replaces a certain part of the string with another string. To use replace, you specify where in the string you want to start the replacement and how many characters you want to replace. Then you specify the replacement string.

For example, if your string is "Something seriously bizarre" and you want to replace "thing" with the string "body", you tell replace() to start at index 4 and replace 5 characters with the word "body". To do this, you enter:

```
words.replace(4, 5, "body");
```

TIP

Notice that the number of characters you replace does not have to be the same as the length of the new string. If the string starts out with "Something seriously bizarre", after this replace() call, the string contains "Somebody seriously bizarre".

Understanding main()

All applications so far in this chapter have had a main(), which is a function. Notice its header, which is followed by code inside braces:

```
int main()
```

You can see that this is definitely a function header: It starts out with a return type and then the function name, main(). This is just one form of main(). However, you may decide that you want to give users the ability to provide input when they type the name of your application at the console. In this case, you use this alternative form of the main() function that includes two parameters:

```
int main(int argc, char *argv[])
```

Notice that the second form of main() has two parameters:

>> int argc: Tells you how many arguments appear on the command line

>> char *argv[]: Provides a list of the command-line arguments in an array

A *command-line argument* is something you type in the Windows Command Prompt or at the macOS or Linux Terminal window after the name of the application (the *command* you want to execute). When you run an application, especially from the command prompt, you type the name of the application and press Enter. But before pressing Enter, you can follow the application name with other words that are generally separated by spaces.

To make these switches and their associated arguments work, the main() function must process the input. You determine how many command-line arguments the user supplied using argc, and then access them using argv. An *array* is a sequence of values stored under one name. The argv variable is one such animal. To access the individual variables stored under the single umbrella known as argv, you do something like this:

```
cout << argv[0] << endl;
```

In this example, you use brackets as you did when accessing the individual characters in a string. You can access the command-line parameters using a *for* loop. The following CommandLine Parameters example demonstrates this technique.

```
#include <iostream>
#include <stdlib.h>

using namespace std;

int main(int argc, char *argv[])
{
  for (int index=1; index < argc; index++)
  {
    cout << argv[index] << endl;
  }

  return 0;
}
```

Chapter **5**

Splitting Up Source Code Files

J ust as you can divide your work into functions, you can divide your work into multiple source code files. The main reason to do so is to help keep your project manageable. Also, with multiple source code files, you can have several people working on a single project, each working on a different source code file at the same time.

In this chapter, you discover how to divide your source code into multiple files (and in all the right places).

Creating Multiple Source Files

If you break the code of your application into multiple source files, put all the files of your application in a separate directory or folder. Then in your command to compile, specify *.cpp to tell the compiler to compile together all the files whose names have the .cpp suffix. One and only one of the source files must contain the main() function. If you add or remove source files, or modify any of them, you'll need to recompile to rebuild your application.

You can put your functions in separate source code files, and they can call each other. In this way, they all work together in the single application. The section "Sharing with Header Files," later in this chapter, shows how you can have a function call another function in a different source file.

You can't break up a single function and put it into two source files. The compiler requires that your functions stay in one piece in a single source file.

After you have multiple files in your project, you can put some of your source in one file and some in another. But before you do, you may want to read some of the other sections in this chapter because they explain how to properly divide your source code.

Before two source files can work together, they must somehow find out about each other. You need to tell each of them about what's in the other file.

When you write a function, normally the function must appear before any calls to it appear within the same source file. That's because of the way the compiler parses the code: If the compiler encounters a call to a function but has not yet heard of that function, it issues an error. But the way around this is to use a function prototype. A *function prototype* is simply the header line from a function, ending with a semicolon, as in the following:

```
void BigDog(int KibblesCount);
```

Later in the source file is the actual function, with this header line duplicated. But instead of a semicolon, the function would have an open brace, the function code, and a closing brace, as in the following:

```
void BigDog(int KibblesCount)
{
   cout << "I'm a lucky dog" << endl;
   cout << "I have " << KibblesCount
        << " pieces of food"
      << endl;
}
```

So, after the function prototype, you can call the function whether the function code itself is before or after the call.

For the compiler to understand a function call, all it needs at the point that the code makes the call is a function *prototype*.

Because the function call needs only a function prototype, you can put the function *itself* in another source code file. You could, therefore, have two separate source code files, as in the MultipleSourceFiles example, shown in Listings 5-1 and 5-2. (The first source code file — main.cpp — is shown in Listing 5-1, and the second source code file — mystuff.cpp — is shown in Listing 5-2.)

LISTING 5-1: Calling a Function with Only a Prototype

```
void BigDog(int KibblesCount);

int main() {
  BigDog(3);
  return 0;
}
```

LISTING 5-2: Using a Function from a Separate File

```
#include <iostream>

using namespace std;

void BigDog(int KibblesCount) {
  cout << "I'm a lucky dog" << endl;
  cout << "I have " << KibblesCount
       << " pieces of food"
    << endl;
}
```

Listings 5-1 and 5-2 break the function away from the prototype. When you compile these two files together as a single application, they all fit together nicely. You can then run the application, and you see this somewhat interesting output:

```
I'm a lucky dog
I have 3 pieces of food
```

Notice that main.cpp doesn't contain either #include <iostream> or using namespace std; because it doesn't have any calls to cout, just the call to BigDog(). You do have to put the #include <iostream> and using namespace std; lines at the start of the mystuff.cpp file because mystuff.cpp does use cout.

Sharing with Header Files

Breaking apart source code into multiple files is easy, but soon you may run into a problem. If you have a function, you would need a prototype for SafeCracker() in every file that calls it. The prototype may look like this:

```
string SafeCracker(int SafeID);
```

But there is an easier way of adding the prototype instead of adding it to every file that uses the function. Simply put this line inside its own file, called a *header file*, and give the filename an .h or .hpp extension. (Most developers use .h.) For this example, you place the line string SafeCracker (int SafeID); in a file called safestuff.h.

Then, instead of typing the header line at the start of each file that needs the function, you type the following:

```
#include "safestuff.h"
```

You would then have the three source code files used for the MultipleSourceFiles2 example, shown in Listings 5-3, 5-4, and 5-5:

>> main.cpp: Calls the function

>> safestuff.h: Contains the function prototype

>> safestuff.cpp: Contains the actual code for the function whose prototype appears in the header file

Lots of files, but now the code is broken into manageable pieces. Also, make sure that you save all three of these files in the same directory or folder.

LISTING 5-3:
Including the Header File in the main File

```
#include <iostream>
#include "safestuff.h"

using namespace std;

int main()
{
  cout << "Surprise, surprise!" << endl;
  cout << "The combination for Safe 12 is: "
       << endl;
  cout << SafeCracker(12) << endl;
  cout << "Let's check on Safe 11 too: " << endl;
  cout << SafeCracker(11) << endl;
  return 0;
}
```

LISTING 5-4:
Containing the Function Prototype in the Header File

```
#ifndef SAFESTUFF_H_INCLUDED
#define SAFESTUFF_H_INCLUDED

using namespace std;

string SafeCracker(int SafeID);

#endif // SAFESTUFF_H_INCLUDED
```

LISTING 5-5:
Containing the Actual Function Code

```
#include <iostream>
using namespace std;

string SafeCracker(int SafeID)
{
  if (SafeID == 12)
```

(continued)

LISTING 5-5: *(continued)*

```
      return "13-26-16";
   else
      return "Safe Combination Unknown";
}
```

Before you compile this application, you need to know a few things about how the compilation process works:

>> When you compile a .cpp file, the compiler outputs a .o (for object) file that is then linked by the linker with all the other .o files to create an executable (Windows will automatically name this with a .exe extension) file. In addition to the .o files from your project, the linker also links in any library files or external code that your application accesses.

>> The compiler doesn't compile the header file into a separate .o file. With the application in Listings 5-3 through 5-5, the compiler creates only two output files: main.o and safestuff.o.

>> When the compiler reads the main.cpp file and reaches the #include "safestuff.h" line for the header file, it verifies that it hasn't read the safestuff.h file before and included it within the .o file.

>> If the safestuff.h file hasn't been read before, the compiler temporarily switches over and reads the header file, pretending that it's still reading the same main.cpp file. As it continues, it compiles everything as if it's all part of the main.cpp file.

REMEMBER

If you include the safestuff.h header file in other source code files, the compiler adds the content to those source files as well. Compile and run the code in Listings 5-3 through 5-5. When you run the application, you see the following output:

```
Surprise, surprise!
The combination for Safe 12 is:
13-26-16
Let's check on Safe 11 too:
Safe Combination Unknown
```

If you have a source file containing some functions, creating a header file that contains the associated function prototypes is generally a good practice. Then you can name the header file the same as the source file, except with a different extension. In this example, you use the safestuff.h file to hold the prototype for the safestuff.cpp file.

Adding the header only once

Adding a header twice is an error because then you'd define the forward reference for a function twice. The section "Using the Mysterious Header Wrappers," later in this chapter, describes how to ensure a header is added only once.

Using angle brackets or quotes

You may have noticed something about the code in Listing 5-3. When including the safestuff.h file, you don't put it inside angle brackets, as with the #include <iostream> line. Instead, you put it inside quotes:

```
#include "safestuff.h"
```

That's because programmers for years have been fighting over the rules of *where* exactly on the hard drive to put the header files. The question is whether to put them in the same directory or folder as your project or to place them in a directory all by themselves.

Regardless of where you put your header files, here is the rule for when to use quotes and when to use brackets: The compiler looks in several directories or folders to find header files. And it can, possibly, look in the same directory as the source file. If you use angle brackets (that is, less-than and greater-than signs), as in #include <string>, the compiler doesn't look in the same directory as the source file. But if you use double quotes, as in #include "safestuff.h", the compiler *first* looks in the same directory or folder as the source file. And if the compiler doesn't find the header file there, it looks in the remaining directories or folders, as it would with angle brackets.

If you start working on a large C++ project, you'll probably find that project managers use the rule of always using angle brackets. For large projects, this is typically the best policy.

TIP

If you try to compile and you get a No such file or directory error on the #include line, it's probably because you put the header file in a source file directory or folder but used angle brackets instead of double quotes. Try switching that line to double quotes.

Sharing Variables among Source Files

When you declare a variable inside a function, it remains local to the function. But you may want functions to share a single *global* variable: One function may store something, and another may read its contents and write it to the console. To do this, declare the global variable outside a function. Declaring the global variable inside a source file works until you try to share it among multiple source files. If you're not careful, the source files end up with a separate copy of the global variable.

There's a trick to making this work. Declare the variable inside one and only one of the source files. Then you declare it *again* inside one (and only one) header file, but you precede it with the word extern, as in extern int DoubleCheeseburgers;.

The GlobalVariable example (shown in Listings 5-6, 5-7, and 5-8) demonstrates the use of a single global variable that is shared among multiple source files.

LISTING 5-6: **Making Use of a Global Variable**

```
#include <iostream>
#include "sharealike.h"

using namespace std;

int main()
{
  DoubleCheeseburgers = 20;
  EatAtJoes();
  return 0;
}
```

```
#ifndef SHAREALIKE_H_INCLUDED
#define SHAREALIKE_H_INCLUDED

extern int DoubleCheeseburgers;
void EatAtJoes();

#endif // SHAREALIKE_H_INCLUDED
```

LISTING 5-8:	Declaring Global Variable Storage in the sharealike.cpp File

```
#include <iostream>
#include "sharealike.h"

using namespace std;

int DoubleCheeseburgers = 0;

void EatAtJoes() {
  cout << "How many cheeseburgers today?"
       << endl;
  cout << DoubleCheeseburgers << endl;
}
```

WARNING

It's a bad idea to declare any variable without initializing it. If you don't initialize the variable, you have no idea what it contains. Not initializing the variable could lead to difficult-to-find errors. Global variables are even worse in this regard because now you don't even have a good idea of precisely where to search.

Using the Mysterious Header Wrappers

When you include a header file, you usually want to include it only *once* per source file. But that can create a problem: Suppose you have a huge software project, and several header files include another of your header files, called superheader.h. If you include all these other header files, how can you be sure to pick up the superheader.h file only once?

The answer looks strange but does the trick. You start each header file with these two lines:

```
#ifndef SHAREALIKE_H_INCLUDED
#define SHAREALIKE_H_INCLUDED
```

Follow these lines with the contents of the header file. Then the last line should be:

```
#endif
```

These *header wrappers*, as they're often called, ensure that the code in the header gets processed only once per source code file each time you compile. The wrappers use special lines called *preprocessor directives*. Basically, the *second* line defines something that is sort of like a variable but is used only during compilation; this something is called a *symbol*. In this case, the symbol is called SHAREALIKE_H_INCLUDED.

The first line checks to see whether this symbol has been defined. If *not*, the compiler proceeds with the lines of code that follow. The next line defines the symbol, so now it's actually defined for later. Then the compiler does all the rest of the lines in the file. Finally, the last line, #endif, simply finishes the very first line.

Now consider what could happen if you include this same file twice, as in the following:

```
#include "sharealike.h"
#include "sharealike.h"
```

The *second* time the compiler goes through sharealike.h, it sees the first line, which checks to see whether the SHAREALIKE_H symbol is defined. But this time it is! So instead of going through all the lines again, the compiler skips to the #endif line that normally appears at the end of the file. Thus, your header file is processed only once per source code file.

When you create a header file, be sure to put the header wrappers around it. You can use any symbol name you like, as long as it uses only letters, numbers, and underscores and doesn't start with a number and isn't already a variable name in your source or a C++ word. But most people base their choice on some variation of the filename itself, such as MYFILE_H or MYFILE_H_ or even _MYFILE_H_.

Using Constants

When you're programming, you may sometimes want a certain fixed value that you plan to use throughout the application. For example, you may want a string containing the name of your company, such as "Bob's Fixit Anywhere Anyhoo". And you don't want someone else working on your application to pass this string into a function as a reference and modify it by mistake. Or, if you're writing a scientific application, you might want a fixed number, such as pi = 3.1415926 or root2 = 1.4142135.

You can create such constants in C++ by using the const keyword. When you create a constant, it works just like a variable, except that you can't change it later in the application. For example, to declare your company name, you might use the following:

```
const string CompanyName = "Bobs Fixit Anywhere
    Anyhoo";
```

Later in your code, you can't do something like this:

```
CompanyName = CompanyName + ", Inc.";
```

The compiler issues an error message for that line, complaining that it's a constant and you can't change it.

After you declare the CompanyName constant, you can use it to refer to your company throughout your code. The Constants example in Listing 5-9 shows you how to do this. Note the three constants toward the top called ParkingSpaces, StoreName, and pi. In the rest of the application, you use these just like any other variables — except that you don't try to change them.

LISTING 5-9: **Using Constants for Permanent Values That Do Not Change**

```cpp
#include <iostream>

using namespace std;

const int ParkingSpaces = 80;
const string StoreName = "Joe's Food Haven";
const float pi = 3.1415926;

int main() {
    cout << "Important Message" << endl;
    cout << "Here at " << StoreName << endl;
    cout << "we believe you should know" << endl;
    cout << "that we have " << ParkingSpaces;
    cout << " full-sized" << endl;
    cout << "parking spaces for your parking"
         << endl;
    cout << "pleasure." << endl;
    cout << endl;
    cout << "We do realize that parking" << endl;
    cout << "is tight at " << StoreName << endl;
    cout << "and so we are going to double our"
         << endl;
    cout << "spaces from " << ParkingSpaces
         << " to ";
    cout << ParkingSpaces * 2;
    cout << ". Thank you again!" << endl << endl;
    float radius = 5;
    float area = radius * radius * pi;
    cout << "And remember, we sell " << radius;
    cout << " inch radius apple pies" << endl;
    cout << "for a full " << area << " square"
         << endl;
    cout << "inches of eating pleasure!" << endl;
    return 0;
}
```

When you run this application, you see the following:

```
Important Message
Here at Joe's Food Haven
we believe you should know
that we have 80 full-sized
parking spaces for your parking
pleasure.

We do realize that parking
is tight at Joe's Food Haven
and so we are going to double our
spaces from 80 to 160. Thank you again!

And remember, we sell 5 radius inch apple pies
for a full 78.5398 square
inches of eating pleasure!
```

TIP

The biggest advantage to using constants is this: If you need to make a change to a string or number throughout your application, you make the change only once. If you have a single constant in the header file for use by all your source code files, you need to change it only *once*. You modify the header file with the new constant definition and recompile your application, and you're ready to go.

Understanding Preprocessor Directives

When you compile an application, the first thing the compiler does is run your code through a preprocessor. The preprocessor simply looks for certain statements in your code that start with the # symbol. You've already seen one such statement in every one of your applications: #include. These preprocessor statements are known as *directives* because they tell the preprocessor to do something — in other words, they direct it. The following sections tell you more about the preprocessor and describe how it works.

Understanding the basics of preprocessing

Think of the preprocessor as just a machine that transforms your code into a temporary, fixed-up version that's all ready to be compiled. For example, look at this preprocessor directive:

```
#include <iostream>
```

If the preprocessor sees this line, it inserts the entire text from the file called iostream (yes, that's a filename; it has no extension) into the fixed-up version of the source code. Suppose that the iostream file looks like this:

```
int hello = 10;
int goodbye = 20;
```

Just two lines are all that's in it. (Of course, the real iostream file is much more sophisticated.) And suppose that your own source file, MyProgram.cpp, has this in it (as found in the Preprocessor example):

```
#include <iostream>

int main()
{
   std::cout << "Hello world!" << std::endl;
   return 0;
}
```

Then, after the preprocessor finishes its preprocessing, it creates a temporary fixed-up file (which has the lines from the iostream file inserted into the MyProgram.cpp file where the #include line had been) to look like this:

```
int hello = 10;
int goodbye = 20;

int main()
{
   std::cout << "Hello world!" << std::endl;
   return 0;
}
```

In other words, the preprocessor replaced the #include line with the contents of that file.

Creating constants with #define

The preprocessor also provides you with a lot of other directives besides #include. One of the more useful ones is the #define directive. Here's a sample #define line:

```
#define MYSPECIALNUMBER 42
```

After the preprocessor sees this line, every time it encounters the word MYSPECIALNUMBER, it replaces it with the word 42 (that is, whatever sequence of letters, numbers, and other characters follow the definition).

Although you can still use #define statements in C++, in general you should simply use a constant instead of a symbol.

Chapter **6**

Referring to Your Data through Pointers

E very little part of the computer's memory is associated with a number that represents its location, or *address*. In this chapter, you see that after you determine the address of a variable stored in memory, you can do powerful things with it, which gives you the tools to create powerful applications.

If any single topic in C++ programming is most important, it is the notion of pointers.

TIP

Considering the Issues with Pointers

A *pointer* is simply an address in memory. The value it contains is the address, and by *dereferencing* the pointer (looking at the address to which it points), you see the value that the pointer references. It's just like the address for your house. You send mail to the address, but the address isn't your house — it's simply a pointer to your house.

The reason for using pointers in the first place is to avoid carrying large objects around in your code. Early applications had to use every tiny bit of memory and CPU processing cycles efficiently or face performance issues. Pointers allowed early applications to perform well simply by pointing at big objects in memory instead of passing them around.

Applications can have invalid pointers, and when the code tries to process this invalid address, it often crashes the application. Of course, the worst problem is the null pointer, 0x000000, which you expect to point to something — but a null pointer points to nothing.

Another problem with pointers is that you spend a lot of time managing them. Every time you work with pointers, you risk:

>> **Creating a memory leak:** By not deallocating the pointer so you can reuse the memory, the memory becomes inaccessible to the application. You could actually run out of memory despite having memory available. The memory becomes available again after the operating system frees it after the application terminates.

>> **Using memory that hasn't been initialized:** The memory location could contain anything and if you act on the data in that memory location, your application will act oddly or simply crash.

>> **Obtaining the wrong data:** The application could point to the wrong location and you may not know it. This means that the application is using the wrong data, which could result in unanticipated output or data damage.

Heaping and Stacking the Variables

C++ applications use two kinds of memory:

>> **Stack:** Each time a function is called, the computer allocates memory for the values of the function's local variables in an area of memory called the *stack*. This memory is automatically deallocated when the function returns.

>> **Heap:** The area in memory shared by the entire program where the computer stores values that the program *dynamically* creates and destroys. These values are accessed via pointers.

Getting a variable's address

Because every variable lives somewhere in memory, every variable has an address. If you have a function that declares an integer variable called NumberOfPotholes, then when your application calls this function, the computer will allocate space for NumberOfPotholes somewhere in memory.

If you want to find the address of the variable NumberOfPotholes, you simply throw an ampersand (&) in front of it. Listing 6-1 shows the VariableAddress example, which obtains the address of a variable and prints it.

REMEMBER

LISTING 6-1: | **Using the & Character to Obtain the Address of a Variable**

```
#include <iostream>

using namespace std;

int main() {
    int NumberOfPotholes = 532587;
    cout << &NumberOfPotholes << endl;
    return 0;
}
```

When you run this application, a hexadecimal number appears on the console. This number may or may not match ours, and it may or may not be the same each time you run the application. When you run Listing 6-1, you see something like the following (it varies with each run):

```
0x22ff74
```

Knowing the address of a variable doesn't tell you about the variable content, but C++ programmers use addresses in other ways:

>> **Modifying the variable content directly using what are called pointer variables:** A *pointer variable* is just like any other variable except that it stores the *address of* another variable.

>> Modifying values pointed at by the address indirectly using any of a number of math techniques.

>> Comparing entities such as objects based on their pointers.

To declare a pointer variable, you need to specify the type of variable it will point to. Then you precede the variable's name with an asterisk, as in the following:

```
int *ptr;
```

This line declares a variable that *points to* an integer. In other words, it can contain the *address* of an integer variable. And how do you grab the address of an integer variable? By using the & notation! Thus, you can do something like this:

```
ptr = &NumberOfPotholes;
```

This line puts the address of the variable NumberOfPotholes in the ptr variable. Remember that ptr doesn't hold the number of potholes; instead, it holds the address of the variable called NumberOfPotholes.

TIP

You specify the type of pointer by the type of item it points to. If a pointer variable points to an integer, its type is *pointer to integer*. In C++ notation, its type is int * (with a space between them) or int* (no space). If a pointer variable points to a string, its type is *pointer to string,* and notation for this type is string *.

REMEMBER

The ptr variable holds an address, but what's at that address? That address is the location in memory of the storage bin known as NumberOfPotholes. Right at that spot in memory is the data stored in NumberOfPotholes.

Changing a variable by using a pointer

After you have a pointer variable holding another variable's address, you can use the pointer to access the information in the other variable. That means you have two ways to get to the information in a variable: Use the variable name itself (such as NumberOfPotholes), or use the pointer variable that points to it.

If you want to store the number 6087 in NumberOfPotholes, you can do this:

```
NumberOfPotholes = 6087;
```

Or you can use the pointer. To use the pointer, you first declare it as follows:

```
ptr = &NumberOfPotholes;
```

Then, to change NumberOfPotholes, you don't just assign a value to it. Instead, you throw an asterisk in front of it, like so:

```
*ptr = 6087;
```

If ptr points to NumberOfPotholes, these two lines of code will have the same effect: Both will change the value to 6087. This process of sticking the asterisk before a pointer variable is called *dereferencing* the pointer. Look at the DereferencePointer example, shown in Listing 6-2, which demonstrates all this.

LISTING 6-2: **Modifying the Original Variable with a Pointer Variable**

```
#include <iostream>

using namespace std;

int main() {
  int NumberOfPotholes;
  int *ptr;

  ptr = &NumberOfPotholes;
  *ptr = 6087;

  cout << NumberOfPotholes << endl;
  return 0;
}
```

In Listing 6-2, the first line of main() declares an integer variable, and the second line declares a pointer to an integer. The next line takes the address of the integer variable and stores it in the pointer. Then the fourth line modifies the original integer by dereferencing the pointer. And just to make sure that the process worked, the next line prints the value of NumberOfPotholes. When you run the application, you see the following output:

```
6087
```

You can also read the value of the original variable through the pointer. Look at the ReadPointer example, shown in Listing 6-3. This code accesses the value of NumberOfPotholes through the pointer variable, ptr. When the code gets the value, it saves it in another variable called SaveForLater.

LISTING 6-3: **Accessing a Value through a Pointer**

```cpp
#include <iostream>

using namespace std;

int main() {
    int NumberOfPotholes;
    int *ptr = &NumberOfPotholes;
    int SaveForLater;

    *ptr = 6087;
    SaveForLater = *ptr;
    cout << SaveForLater << endl;

    *ptr = 7000;
    cout << *ptr << endl;
    cout << SaveForLater << endl;
    return 0;
}
```

When you run this application, you see the following output:

```
6087
7000
6087
```

Notice that the code changes the value through ptr again — this time to 7000. When you run the application, you can see that the value did, indeed, change, but the value in SaveForLater remained the same. That's because SaveForLater is a separate variable, not connected to the other two. The other two, however, are connected to each other.

Pointing at a string

Pointer variables can point to any type, including strings. However, after you say that a variable points to a certain type, it can point to only that type. That is, as with any variable, you can't change its type. The compiler won't let you do it.

To create a pointer to a string, you simply make the type of the variable string *. You can then set it equal to the address of a string variable. The StringPointer example, shown in Listing 6-4, demonstrates this idea.

LISTING 6-4:   **Pointing to a String with Pointers**

```
#include <iostream>

using namespace std;

int main() {
    string GoodMovie;
    string *ptrToString;

    GoodMovie = "Best in Show";
    ptrToString = &GoodMovie;

    cout << *ptrToString << endl;
    return 0;
}
```

In Listing 6-4, you see that the pointer named ptrToString points to the variable named GoodMovie. But when you want to use the pointer to access the string, you need to dereference the pointer by putting an asterisk (*) in front of it. When you run this code, you see the results of the dereferenced pointer, which is the value of the GoodMovie variable:

```
Best in Show
```

You can change the value of the string through the pointer, again by dereferencing it, as in the following code:

```
*ptrToString = "Galaxy Quest";
cout << GoodMovie << endl;
```

The code dereferences the pointer to set it equal to the string "GalaxyQuest". Then, to show that it truly changed, the code prints the GoodMovie variable. The result of this code, when added at the end of Listing 6-4 (but prior to the return 0), is

```
Galaxy Quest
```

You can also use the pointer to access the individual parts of the string, as shown in the StringPointer2 example in Listing 6-5.

LISTING 6-5: **Using Pointers to Point to a String**

```
#include <iostream>

using namespace std;

int main() {
    string AMovie;
    string *ptrToString;

    AMovie = "L.A. Confidential";
    ptrToString = &AMovie;

    for (unsigned i = 0; i < AMovie.length(); i++)
    {
        cout << (*ptrToString)[i] << " ";
    }
    cout << endl;

    return 0;
}
```

When you run this application, you see the letters of the movie appear with spaces between them, as in

```
L . A .  C o n f i d e n t i a l
```

WARNING

When you access the characters of the string through a pointer, you need to put parentheses around the asterisk and the pointer variable.

This application loops through the entire string, character by character. The string's length() function tells how many characters are in the string. The code inside the loop grabs the individual characters and prints them with a space after each.

Notice that i is of type unsigned rather than int. The length() function returns an unsigned value rather than an int value, which makes sense because a string can't have a negative length. If you try to use an int for i, the compiler displays the following warning:

```
warning: comparison between signed and
    unsigned integer
```

The application still runs, but you need to use the correct data types for loop variables. Otherwise, when the loop value increases over the amount that the loop variable can support, the application will fail. Trying to find such an error can prove frustrating even for the best developers. Don't ignore warnings, even if they appear harmless.

TIP

You can also change the individual characters in a string through a pointer. You can do this by using a line like (*ptrToString)[5] = 'X';. Notice you still need to put parentheses around the variable name along with the dereferencing character.

TIP

The length of a string is also available through the pointer. You can call the length() function by dereferencing the pointer, again with the carefully placed parentheses, such as in the following:

```
for (unsigned i = 0; i < (*ptrToString).length();
    i++)
{
   cout << (*ptrToString)[i] << " ";
}
```

Pointing to something else

When you create a pointer variable, you must specify the type of data it points to. After that, you can't change the type of data it points to, but you can change *what* it points to. For example, if you have a pointer to an integer, you can make it point to the integer variable called ExpensiveComputer. Then, later, in the same application, you can make it point to the integer variable called CheapComputer. Listing 6-6 demonstrates this technique in the ChangePointer example.

LISTING 6-6: Using Pointers to Point to Something Else and Back Again

```cpp
#include <iostream>

using namespace std;

int main() {
    int ExpensiveComputer;
    int CheapComputer;
    int *ptrToComp;

    ptrToComp = &ExpensiveComputer;
    *ptrToComp = 2000;
    cout << *ptrToComp << endl;

    ptrToComp = &CheapComputer;
    *ptrToComp = 500;
    cout << *ptrToComp << endl;

    ptrToComp = &ExpensiveComputer;
    cout << *ptrToComp << endl;
    return 0;
}
```

This code starts out by initializing two integers and a pointer to an integer.

Next, the code points the pointer to ExpensiveComputer and uses the pointer to put 2000 inside ExpensiveComputer. Then the code changes what the pointer points to.

Be careful if you use one pointer to bounce around several different variables. You can easily lose track of which variable the pointer is pointing to.

Getting tips on pointer variables

You can declare two pointer variables of the same type by putting them together in a single statement, as you can with regular variables. However, you must precede *each one* with an asterisk, as in the following line:

```
int *ptrOne, *ptrTwo;
```

If you try to declare multiple pointers on a single line but put an asterisk only before the first pointer, only that one will be a pointer. The rest will not be. This can cause serious headaches later because this line compiles fine:

```
int *ptrOne, Confused;
```

Here, Confused is not a pointer to an integer; instead, it's just an integer. Beware!

Some people like to put the asterisk immediately after the type, as in the following example, to emphasize the fact that the type is *pointer to integer:*

```
int* ptrOne;
```

But this approach makes it easy to leave out the asterisks for any pointer variables that follow.

Creating New Pointers

It isn't possible to predict some kinds of memory use in your application, but the requirements aren't known when you write the code. For example, streaming data from the internet or creating new records in a database are both examples of unpredictable memory use. When working with unpredictable memory requirements, you *allocate* (request memory) and *deallocate* (release the memory you requested) as needed in a process called *dynamic memory management.* You use the *heap,* an area of unallocated memory, to perform dynamic memory management.

Using new

To declare a value on the heap using existing methods, first you need to set up a variable that will help you keep track of the storage bin. This variable must be a pointer variable.

To allocate memory on the heap, you need to do two things: First, declare a pointer variable. Second, use the *new* operator by specifying the type of value you want to create. For example, the following line creates a new integer value:

```
int *somewhere = new int;
```

After the computer creates the new integer value on the heap, it stores the address of the integer value in somewhere. And that makes sense: somewhere is a pointer to an integer, so it's prefaced by the * (pointer) operator. Thus, somewhere holds the address of an integer value. The UseNew example, shown in Listing 6-7, demonstrates how pointers work when using new.

LISTING 6-7: **Allocating Memory by Using new**

```cpp
#include <iostream>

using namespace std;

int main() {
    int *ptr = new int;
    *ptr = 10;
    cout << *ptr << endl;
    cout << ptr << endl;
    return 0;
}
```

When you run this application, you see this output (the second value will change each time you run the example):

```
10
0x73af10
```

In this application, you first allocate a pointer variable, which you call ptr. Then you call new with an int type, which returns a pointer to an integer. You save that return value in the ptr variable.

You save a 10 in the memory that ptr points to. And then you print the value stored in the memory that ptr points to.

To see for yourself that ptr is pointing to a memory location and not the actual value of 10, the code also prints ptr without *dereferencing* it (using the * operator). The output is a hexadecimal value such as 0x9caef0, but this output will change each time because the memory allocation occurs in a different location on the heap each time.

As you can see, ptr contains the address of the value allocated by the new operator. The only way you can access it is through the pointer.

REMEMBER

When you call new, you get back a pointer. This pointer is of the type that you specify in your call to new. You can then store the pointer only in a pointer variable of the same type.

TIP

When you use the new operator, the usual terminology is that you are *allocating memory on the heap.*

By using pointers to access memory on the heap, you can take advantage of many interesting C++ features. For example, you can use pointers along with something called an array. An *array* is simply a large storage bin that has multiple slots, each of which holds one item. (Chapter 8 discusses arrays.) If you set up an array that holds pointers, you can store all these pointers without having to name them individually. And these pointers can point to complex things, called *objects.* You could then pass all these variables (which could be quite large, if they're strings) to a function by passing only the array, not the strings themselves. That step saves memory on the stack.

In addition to objects and arrays, you can have a function allocate memory and return a variable pointing to that memory. Then, when you get the variable back from the function, you can use it, and when you finish with the variable, delete it (freeing the memory). Finally, you can pass a pointer into a function. When you do so, the function can actually modify the data the pointer references for you. (See "Passing Pointer Variables to Functions" and "Returning Pointer Variables from Functions," later in this chapter for details.)

Using an initializer

When you call new, you can provide an initial value for the memory you're allocating. For example, when allocating a new integer, you can also store the number 10 in the integer. The Initializer example shown in Listing 6-8 demonstrates how to do this.

LISTING 6-8: **Putting a Value in Parentheses to Initialize Memory That You Allocate**

```
#include <iostream>

using namespace std;

int main() {
  int *ptr = new int(10);
  cout << *ptr << endl;
  return 0;
}
```

This code calls new, but it also provides a number in parentheses. That number is put in the memory initially, instead of being assigned to it later. This line of code is equivalent to the following two lines of code:

```
int *ptr = new int;
*ptr = 10;
```

Freeing Pointers

When you allocate memory on the heap by calling the new operator and you're finished using the memory, you need to let the computer know, regardless of whether it's just a little bit of memory or a lot. The computer doesn't look ahead into your code to find out whether you're still going to use the memory. So, in your code, when you're finished with the memory, you *free* the memory.

The way you free the memory is by calling the `delete` operator and passing the name of the pointer:

```
delete MyPointer;
```

This line would appear after you're finished using a pointer that you allocated by using `new`.

The `FreePointer` example, shown in Listing 6-9, provides a complete demonstration of allocating a pointer, using it, and then freeing it. Note the use of the `replace()` method, which first appears in the "Replacing parts of a string" section of Chapter 4. You use the arrow operator (->) to access this `string` method of `phrase`. For now, consider the following:

```
phrase->(22, 4, "oked")
```

To be shorthand for

```
(*phrase).(22, 4, "oked")
```

The "Using classes and pointers" section of Chapter 7 describes the arrow operator in more detail.

LISTING 6-9: Using delete to Clean Up Your Pointers

```
#include <iostream>

using namespace std;

int main() {
  string *phrase =
    new string("All presidents are cool!!!");
  cout << *phrase << endl;

  (*phrase)[20] = 'r';
  phrase->replace(22, 4, "oked");
  cout << *phrase << endl;

  delete phrase;
  return 0;
}
```

When you run this application, you see the following output:

```
All presidents are cool!!!
All presidents are crooked
```

This code allocates a new string and initializes it, saving its address in the pointer variable called phrase. The code outputs the phrase, manipulates it, and then writes it again. Finally, the code frees the memory used by the phrase.

TIP

Although people usually say that you're *deleting the pointer* or *freeing the pointer*, you're actually freeing the *memory* that the pointer points to. The pointer can still be used for subsequent new operations.

WARNING

When you free memory, the memory becomes available for other tasks. However, immediately after the call to delete, the pointer still points to that particular memory location, even though the memory is free. Using the pointer without pointing it to something else causes errors. Therefore, don't try to use the pointer after freeing the memory it points to until you set the pointer to point to something else through a call to new or by setting it to another variable.

Whenever you free a pointer, a good habit is to set the pointer to nullptr. Then, whenever you use a pointer, first check whether it's equal to nullptr and use it only if it's not nullptr.

The following code sample shows how to use this strategy. First, this code frees the pointer; then it clears the pointer by setting it to 0:

```
delete ptrToSomething;
ptrToSomething = nullptr;
```

This code checks whether the pointer is not nullptr before using it:

```
ptrToComp = new int;
*ptrToComp = 10;
```

```
if (ptrToComp != nullptr) {
    cout << *ptrToComp << endl;
}
```

WARNING

Call `delete` only on memory that you allocated by using `new`. You can free only memory on the heap, not local variables on the stack. In addition, you should avoid freeing the same pointer multiple times because doing so can create hard-to-find bugs; the application may have already reallocated that memory for some other purpose.

WARNING

An older method of freeing a pointer involves setting the pointer to `NULL`. You may have a lot of older code that uses `NULL`. In this case, you must add `#include <cstddef>` to your code to allow it to compile. However, it would be better to update the code to use `nullptr`.

WARNING

The important thing to remember about copying pointers is that copying a pointer only copies the pointer address, not the underlying reference. So, if you copy a pointer to an array, there is still just one array, but now you have two references to that array. To create a copy of an array, you would need to create a second array of the same size and copy the data, index by index, from the first array to the second array.

Passing Pointer Variables to Functions

One of the most important uses for pointers is this: If a pointer points to a variable, you can pass the pointer to a function, and the function can modify the original variable. This functionality lets you write functions that can actually modify the variables passed to them. Even though this section discusses raw pointers, the same techniques work with smart pointers.

Normally, when you call a function and you pass a few variables to the function, the computer just grabs the values out of the variables and passes those values. Take a close look at the Variable Pointer example, shown in Listing 6-10.

LISTING 6-10: **A Function Cannot Change the Original Variables Passed into It**

```cpp
#include <iostream>

using namespace std;

void ChangesAreGood(int myparam) {
  myparam += 10;
  cout << "Inside the function:" << endl;
  cout << myparam << endl;
}

int main() {
  int mynumber = 30;
  cout << "Before the function:" << endl;
  cout << mynumber << endl;

  ChangesAreGood(mynumber);
  cout << "After the function:" << endl;
  cout << mynumber << endl;

  return 0;
}
```

Listing 6-10 includes a function called ChangesAreGood() that modifies the parameter it receives. (It adds 10 to its parameter called myparam.) It then prints the new value of the parameter.

The main() function initializes an integer variable, mynumber, to 30 and prints its value. It then calls the ChangesAreGood() function, which changes its parameter. After coming back from the ChangesAreGood() function, main() prints the value again. When you run this application, you see the following output:

```
Before the function:
30
Inside the function:
40
After the function:
30
```

Before the function call, `mynumber` is 30. And after the function call, it's still 30. But the function added 10 to its parameter. This means that when the function modified its parameter, the original variable remained untouched. The two are separate entities. Only the value 30 went into the function. The actual variable did not. It stayed in `main()`. But what if you write a function that you *want* to modify the original variable?

A pointer contains a number, which represents the address of a variable. If you pass this address into a function and the function stores that address into one of its own variables, its own variable also points to the same variable that the original pointer did. The pointer variable in `main()` and the pointer variable in the function both point to the same variable because both pointers hold the same address.

That's how you let a function modify data in a variable: You pass a pointer. But when you call a function, the process is easy because you don't need to make a pointer variable. Instead, you can just call the function, putting an ampersand (&) in front of the variable. Then you're not passing the variable or its value — instead, you're passing the address of the variable.

The `VariablePointer2` example, shown in Listing 6-11, is a modified form of Listing 6-10; this time, the function actually manages to modify the original variable.

LISTING 6-11: Using Pointers to Modify a Variable Passed into a Function

```
#include <iostream>

using namespace std;

void ChangesAreGood(int *myparam) {
  *myparam += 10;
  cout << "Inside the function:" << endl;
  cout << *myparam << endl;
}

int main() {
  int mynumber = 30;
```

(continued)

LISTING 6-11: *(continued)*

```
cout << "Before the function:" << endl;
cout << mynumber << endl;

ChangesAreGood(&mynumber);
cout << "After the function:" << endl;
cout << mynumber << endl;

return 0;
}
```

When you run this application, you see the following output:

```
Before the function:
30
Inside the function:
40
After the function:
40
```

Notice the important difference between this and the output from Listing 6-10: The final line of output is 40, not 30. The variable was modified by the function!

To understand how this happened, first look at main(). The only difference in main() is that it has an ampersand (&) in front of the mynumber argument in the call to ChangesAreGood(). ChangesAreGood() receives the address of mynumber.

Now the function has some major changes. The function header takes a pointer rather than a number. You perform this task by adding an asterisk (*) so that the parameter is a pointer variable. This pointer receives the address being passed into it. Thus, it points to the variable mynumber. Therefore, any modifications made by dereferencing the pointer will change the original variable. The following line changes the original variable.

```
(*myparam) += 10;
```

The ChangesAreGood() function in Listing 6-11 no longer modifies its own parameter. The parameter holds the address of the original mynumber variable, and that never changes. Throughout the function, the pointer variable myparam holds the mynumber address. And any changes the function performs are on the dereferenced variable, which is mynumber.

Returning Pointer Variables from Functions

Functions can return values, including pointers. To set up a function to return a pointer, specify the type followed by an asterisk at the beginning of the function header. The ReturnPointer example, shown in Listing 6-12, demonstrates this technique. The function returns a pointer that is the result of a new operation.

LISTING 6-12: **Returning a Pointer from a String Involves Using an Asterisk in the Return Type**

```
#include <iostream>
#include <sstream>
#include <stdlib.h>

using namespace std;

string *GetSecretCode() {
    string *code = new string;
    code->append("CR");

    int randomnumber = rand();
    ostringstream converter;
    converter << randomnumber;
    code->append(converter.str());

    code->append("NQ");
    return code;
}

int main() {
    string *newcode;
```

(continued)

LISTING 6-12: *(continued)*

```
for (int index = 0; index < 5; index++) {
    newcode = GetSecretCode();
    cout << *newcode << endl;
}

return 0;
}
```

The main() function creates a pointer to a string named newcode. GetSecretCode() returns a pointer to a string, so newcode and the function return value match. When you use newcode, you must dereference it.

When you run this application, you see something like the following output:

```
CR41NQ
CR18467NQ
CR6334NQ
CR26500NQ
CR19169NQ
```

WARNING

Never return from a function the address of a local variable in the function. The local variables live in the stack space allocated for the function, not in the heap. When the function is finished, the computer frees the stack space used for the function, making room for the *next* function call. If you try this, the variables will be okay for a while, but after enough function calls follow, the variable's data will get overwritten.

Just as the parameters to a function are normally values, a function normally *returns* a value. In the case of returning a pointer, the function is still returning just a value — it's returning the value of the pointer, which is a number representing an address.

Chapter **7**

Working with Classes

B ack in the early 1990s, the big buzzword in the computer world was *object-oriented*. For anything to sell, it had to be object-oriented. Programming languages were object-oriented. Software applications were object-oriented. Computers were object-oriented. Unfortunately, object-oriented was simply a cool catchphrase at the time that meant little in real terms. Often, ideas begin poorly formed and gain resolution as people work to implement the idea in the real world.

Now it's possible to explore what object-oriented *really* means and how you can use it to organize your C++ applications. In this chapter, you discover object-oriented programming and see how you can do it in C++. Although people disagree on the strict definition of *object-oriented*, in this book it means "programming with objects and classes."

Understanding Objects and Classes

When describing what objects can do, you carefully write it from the perspective of the object itself, not from the perspective of the person *using* the object. A good way to name the capability is to test it by preceding it with the words *I can* and see if it makes sense. Thus, because "I can *write on paper*" works from the perspective of a pen, the list contains *write on paper* for one of the pen's capabilities.

But is seeing all the objects in the universe possible, or are some objects hidden? Certainly, some objects are physical, like atoms or the dark side of the moon, and you can't see them. But other objects are abstract. For example, you may have a credit card account. What is a credit card account, exactly? A credit card account is abstract because you can't touch it — it has no physical presence. The following sections examine various kinds of objects.

Classifying classes and objects

When you see a pen, you may ask what *class* this *object* belongs to. If you then pick up another pen, you see another example of the same class. One class; several examples.

So, when you organize things, you specify a *class*, which is the type of object. You can start picking out examples (or *instances*) of the class. Each class may have several instances.

Describing properties and behaviors

If you choose a class, you can describe its characteristics. You're listing only general characteristics for all instances of the class Pen. That is, every pen has these properties. But the actual values for these properties may vary from instance to instance. One pen may have a different ink color from another, but both may have the same brand. Nevertheless, they're both separate instances of the class Pen.

All the pens in the class share properties. But the values for these properties may differ from pen to pen. When you *instantiate* (build or create) a new Pen, you follow the list of properties, giving the new pen instance its own values.

But all these pens have the same *behaviors:*

>> **Behavior #1:** Write on paper

>> **Behavior #2:** Break in half

>> **Behavior #3:** Run out of ink

Unlike properties, behaviors don't change from instance to instance. They're the same for each class.

When you describe classes to build a computer application using a class, you're modeling. In the preceding examples, you modeled a class called Pen.

Implementing a class

To implement a class in C++, you use the keyword class. And then you add the name of the class, such as Pen. You then add an open brace, list your properties and behaviors, and end with a closing brace.

Most people capitalize the first letter of a class name in C++, and if their class name is a word, they don't capitalize the remaining letters. Although you don't have to follow this rule, many people do. You can choose any name for a C++ class provided it isn't a C++ keyword; it consists only of letters, digits, and underscores; and it doesn't start with a number.

The PenClass example, shown in Listing 7-1, contains a C++ class description that appears inside the Pen.h header file. The "Accessing members" section later in this chapter explains the word public.

You can create several *objects* (also called *instances*) of a single class. Each object gets its own properties, which you declare in the class. To access the members of an object, you use a period (or dot).

Separating member function code

When you work with functions, you can either make sure that the code to your function is positioned before any calls to the function, or you can use a *forward reference,* also called a *function prototype* (see Chapter 4).

When you work with classes and member functions, you have a similar option. Most C++ programmers prefer to keep the code for their member functions outside the class definition. The reason for placing them outside is to make the code easier to read; you don't end up with a single, huge block of code that's incredibly difficult to follow. In addition, someone using the class may not care about how the member functions are coded, so keeping their implementations separate is the best option. The class definition contains member function prototypes. If the function is one or two lines of code, people may leave it in the class definition.

A member function prototype would look like this:

```
void break_in_half();
```

Listing 7-1 shows the header file Pen.h for class Pen.

LISTING 7-1: **Using Member Function Prototypes within Header File Pen.h**

```
#ifndef PEN_H_INCLUDED
#define PEN_H_INCLUDED

using namespace std;
enum Color {
  blue,
  red,
  black,
  clear,
  grey
};

enum PenStyle {
  ballpoint,
  felt_tip,
  fountain_pen
};

class Pen {
public:
    Color InkColor;
    Color ShellColor;
    Color CapColor;
    PenStyle Style;
    float Length;
    string Brand;
    int InkLevelPercent;

    void write_on_paper(string words);
    void break_in_half();
    void run_out_of_ink();
};

#endif // PEN_H_INCLUDED
```

After you write a class's member function prototype in the header file, you write the member function code outside the class definition in a separate *implementation file*. However, you need to throw in the name of the class, so that the compiler knows which class this function goes with. You separate the class name and function name with a *scope resolution operator* (::) that links the functions to the class:

```
void Pen::break_in_half() {
    InkLevelPercent = InkLevelPercent / 2;
    Length = Length / 2.0;
}
```

TIP

You can use the same member function name in different classes. As are variables in different functions, member function names are associated with a particular class using the scope resolution operator. Although you don't want to go overboard on duplicating function names, if you feel the need to, you can certainly do it without a problem. For example, toString() is a common function name, and you often see it provided with a wide range of classes in your application.

Listings 7-2 shows the implementation file Pen.cpp, which has the code that implements each member function of class Pen.

LISTING 7-2: **Implementing the Member Functions of Class Pen in Pen.cpp**

```
#include <iostream>
#include "Pen.h"

using namespace std;

void Pen::write_on_paper(string words) {
  if (InkLevelPercent <= 0) {
    cout << "Oops! Out of ink!" << endl;
  }
  else {
    cout << words << endl;
    InkLevelPercent = InkLevelPercent
                    - words.length();
  }
```

(continued)

LISTING 7-2: *(continued)*

```
}

void Pen::break_in_half() {
  InkLevelPercent = InkLevelPercent / 2;
  Length = Length / 2.0;
}

void Pen::run_out_of_ink() {
  InkLevelPercent = 0;
}
```

Member function `Pen::write_on_paper()` uses member variable `InkLevelPercent`, which was declared in header file `Pen.h`. Suppose you call this member function for two different objects, as in the following:

```
FavoritePen.write_on_paper("Hello I am a pen");
WorstPen.write_on_paper(
                "Hello I am another pen");
```

The first of these lines calls `write_on_paper()` for the `FavoritePen` object; thus, inside the code for `write_on_paper()`, the `InkLevelPercent` refers to `InkLevelPercent` for the `FavoritePen` object. But `WorstPen` has its *own* `InkLevelPercent` property, separate from that of `FavoritePen`. So in the second of these two lines, `write_on_paper()` accesses the `InkLevel Percent` that lives inside `WorstPen`. In other words, each object has its own `InkLevelPercent`. When you call `write_on_paper()`, the member function modifies the member variable based on which object you're calling it with. The first line calls it with `FavoritePen`. The second line calls it with `WorstPen`.

We've implemented all the member functions from the class in a separate source (`.cpp`) file. The header file now just lists prototypes and is easier to read. The source file includes the header file at the top. That's required; otherwise, the compiler won't know that `Pen` is a class name.

Listing 7-3 is source file `main.cpp` that uses class Pen.

LISTING 7-3: **main.cpp Contains Code That Uses the Class Pen**

```cpp
#include <iostream>
#include "Pen.h"

using namespace std;

int main() {
    Pen FavoritePen;
    FavoritePen.InkColor = blue;
    FavoritePen.ShellColor = grey;
    FavoritePen.CapColor = blue;
    FavoritePen.Style = ballpoint;
    FavoritePen.Length = 5.5;
    FavoritePen.Brand = "Office Depot";
    FavoritePen.InkLevelPercent = 30;

    Pen WorstPen;
    WorstPen.InkColor = red;
    WorstPen.ShellColor = red;
    WorstPen.CapColor = black;
    WorstPen.Style = fountain_pen;
    WorstPen.Length = 5.0;
    WorstPen.Brand = "Parker";
    WorstPen.InkLevelPercent = 60;

    cout << "This is my favorite pen" << endl;
    cout << "Color: " << FavoritePen.InkColor
        << endl;
    cout << "Brand: " << FavoritePen.Brand << endl;
    cout << "Ink Level: "
        << FavoritePen.InkLevelPercent
        << "%" << endl;
    FavoritePen.write_on_paper("Hello I am a pen");
    cout << "Ink Level: "
        << FavoritePen.InkLevelPercent
        << "%" << endl;

    return 0;
}
```

There are two variables of class Pen: FavoritePen and WorstPen. To access the properties of these objects, you type the name of the variable holding the object, a dot, and then the member variable. For example, to access the InkLevelPercent member of WorstPen, you type the following:

```
WorstPen.InkLevelPercent = 60;
```

You can also run some of the member functions that are in these objects. This code calls:

```
FavoritePen.write_on_paper("Hello I am a pen");
```

This called the function write_on_paper() for the object FavoritePen.

The output of the program is

```
This is my favorite pen
Color: 0
Brand: Office Depot
Ink Level: 30%
Hello I am a pen
Ink Level: 14%
```

You should notice something about the color line. Here's the line of code that writes it:

```
cout << "Color: " << FavoritePen.InkColor << endl;
```

This line outputs the InkColor member for FavoritePen. But what type is InkColor? It's the new Color enumerated type. The property's value was set by the assignment statement:

```
FavoritePen.InkColor = blue;
```

As explained in Chapter 2, the enumeration value blue is stored as integer 0, so the cout statement prints "Color: 0".

REMEMBER

You can create several *objects* (also called *instances*) of a single class. Each object gets its own properties, which you declare in the class. To access the members of an object, you use a period (or dot).

Identifying the parts of a class

Here's a summary of the parts of a class and the different ways classes can work together:

- **Class:** A *class* is a type. It includes member variables to specify its properties and member functions to define its behaviors.

- **Object:** An *object* is an instance of a class.

- **Class definition:** The *class definition* describes the class. It starts with the word class and then has the name of the class, followed by an open brace and closing brace. Inside the braces are the members of the class.

- **Property:** A *property* is a characteristic of a class, such as a color, style, or other descriptive element. You use member variables to specify the properties. Each instance of the class gets its own copy of each property.

- **Behavior:** A *behavior* of a class is a task that an instance of the class can perform. You define each behavior with a member function. When you call a member function for a particular instance, the member function accesses the member variables for the instance.

When you divide the class, you put part in the header file and part in the source code file. The following list describes what goes where:

- **Header file:** Put the class definition in the header file. Member variables appear as part of the class definition within the header. You can include the code for a member function inside the class definition if it's a short function, but most people prefer to have only prototypes of the member functions. You may want to name the header file the same as the class but with an .h or .hpp extension.

- **Source file:** If your class definition contained member function prototypes you need to put the function code in a source file. When you do, precede the function name with the class name and the scope resolution operator (::). If you named the header file the same as the class, you probably want to name the source file the same as the class as well but with a .cpp extension.

Working with a Class

In this section, you explore several clever ways of working with classes, starting with the way you can hide certain parts of your class from other functions that are accessing them.

Accessing members

When you work with an object in real life, there are often parts of the object that you interact with and other parts that you don't. For example, when you use the computer, you type on the keyboard but don't open the box and poke around with a wire attached to a battery. For the most part, the stuff inside is off-limits except when you're upgrading it.

In object terminology, the words *public* and *private* refer to members of a class. When you design a class, you may want to make some member variables and functions freely accessible by class users. You may want to keep other members tucked away. A *class user* is the part of an application that creates an instance of a class and calls one of its member functions.

When designing a class, you may want only specific users calling certain member functions. You may want to keep other member functions hidden away, to be called only by other member functions within the class.

REMEMBER

You bar users from calling member functions by making them *private*. Member functions that you want to allow access to you make *public*. After you design a class, if you write a function that instantiates an object of that class and try to call one of an object's private member functions, you get a compiler error when you try to compile it.

The `OvenClass` example, shown in Listing 7-4, defines a sample `Oven` class and a `main()` that uses it. Look at the class definition. It has two sections: one private and the other public. The code for the member functions appears after the class definition. The two private member functions don't do much other than print a message, although they're also free to call other private functions in the class. The public member function, `Bake()` is allowed to call each of the private functions.

LISTING 7-4: **Using the Public and Private Words to Hide Parts of Your Class**

```cpp
#include <iostream>

using namespace std;

class Oven {
private:
  void TurnOnHeatingElement();
  void TurnOffHeatingElement();
public:
  void Bake(int Temperature);
};

void Oven::TurnOnHeatingElement() {
  cout << "Heating element is now ON!
      Be careful!" << endl;
}

void Oven::TurnOffHeatingElement() {
  cout << "Heating element is now off. Relax!"
      << endl;
}

void Oven::Bake(int Temperature) {
  TurnOnHeatingElement();
  cout << "Baking!" << endl;
  TurnOffHeatingElement();
}

int main() {
  Oven fred;
  fred.Bake(875);
  return 0;
}
```

When you run this application, you see some messages:

```
Heating element is now ON! Be careful!
Baking!
Heating element is now off. Relax!
```

If you included the following line in your `main()` that tries to call a private member function:

```
fred.TurnOnHeatingElement();
```

You would get an error message telling you that you can't do it because the function is private.

When you design your classes, consider making all its members private by default, and then only make those public that you want users to access. This approach allows you to "hide" members that other applications don't need to access.

Using classes and pointers

As with any variable, you can have a pointer variable that points to an object. As usual, the pointer variable's type must match the type of the class. This creates a pointer variable that points to a Pen instance:

```
Pen *MyPen;
```

The variable MyPen is a pointer, and it can point to an object of type Pen. The variable's own type is pointer to Pen, or in C++ notation, Pen *.

A line of code like Pen *MyPen; creates a variable that serves as a pointer to an object. To create an instance, you have to call new.

After you create the variable MyPen, you can create an instance of class Pen and point MyPen to it using the new keyword, like so:

```
MyPen = new Pen;
```

Or you can combine both Pen *MyPen; and the preceding line:

```
Pen *MyPen = new Pen;
```

Now you have the object in the heap. (See Chapter 6 for more information on pointers and heaps.) You also have the pointer variable, which points to the object. Because the object is in the heap, the only way to access it is through the pointer. To access the members through the pointer, you use the *arrow operator:*

```
MyPen->InkColor = red;
```

This goes through the MyPen pointer to set the InkColor property of the object to red. The arrow operator is shorthand for the following:

```
(*MyPen).InkColor = red;
```

Most programmers prefer to use the arrow operator.

As with other values you created with new, after you're finished using an object, you should call delete to free the memory used by the object pointed to by MyPen. To do so, start with the word delete and then the name of the object pointer, MyPen, as in the following:

```
delete MyPen;
```

Store nullptr in the pointer after you delete the object it points to. When you call delete on a pointer to an object, you're deleting the object itself, not the pointer. If you don't store a nullptr in the pointer, it still points to where the object *used to be.*

The PenClass3 example, shown in Listing 7-5, demonstrates the process of declaring a pointer, creating an object and pointing to it, accessing the object's members through the pointer, deleting the object, and clearing the pointer back to 0.

LISTING 7-5: **Managing an Object's Life**

```
#include <iostream>
#include "../PenClass2/Pen.h"

using namespace std;

int main() {
  Pen *MyPen;
  MyPen = new Pen;
  MyPen->InkColor = red;
  cout << MyPen->InkColor << endl;
  delete MyPen;
  MyPen = nullptr;
  return 0;
}
```

The following steps describe precisely how to work with pointers and objects:

1. **Declare the pointer.**

   The pointer must match the type of object you intend to work with, except that the pointer's type name in C++ is followed by an asterisk (*).

2. **Call** new, **passing the class name, and store the results of** new **in the pointer.**

   You can combine Steps 1 and 2 into a single step.

3. **Access the object's members through the pointer with the arrow operator (–>).**

4. **When you're finished with the object, call** delete.

   This step frees the object from the heap. Remember that this doesn't delete the pointer itself — it just frees the object memory.

5. **Clear the pointer by setting it to** nullptr.

Passing objects to functions

When you write a function, normally you base your decision about using pointers on whether you want to change the original variables passed into the function. Suppose you have a function called AddOne( ), and it takes an integer as a parameter. If you want to modify the original variable, you can use a pointer (or you can use a reference). If you don't want to modify the variable, just pass the variable *by value.*

The following prototype represents a function that can modify the variable passed into it:

```
void AddOne( int *number );
```

And this prototype represents a function that cannot modify the variable passed into it:

```
void AddOne( int number );
```

With objects, you can do something similar. For example, this function takes a pointer to an object and can, therefore, modify the object:

```
void FixFlatTire(Car *mycar);
```

This version doesn't allow modification of the original object:

```
void FixFlatTire(Car mycar);
```

Every time you call this function, it creates an entirely new instance of class Car. This instance would be a duplicate copy of the myCar object that is an instance of class Car — it wouldn't be the same instance.

TIP

The smart move with objects is to always pass objects as pointers. Don't pass objects directly into functions. Yes, it risks bad code changing the object, but careful C++ programmers want the actual object, not a copy. Having access to the original outweighs the risk of an accidental change. This chapter explains how to prevent accidental changes by using the const parameters in the next section.

Because your function receives its objects as pointers, you continue accessing them by using the arrow operator. For example, the function FixFlatTire() may do this:

```
void FixFlatTire(Car *mycar) {
    mycar->RemoveTire();
    mycar->AddNewTire();
}
```

Or, if you prefer references, you would do this:

```
void FixFlatTire2(Car &mycar) {
    mycar.RemoveTire();
    mycar.AddNewTire();
}
```

REMEMBER

Pointers contain the address of an object, while a reference is simply another name (or an *alias*) for an object. Even though the reference is still an address, it's the actual address of the object, rather than a pointer to the object. (Chapter 6 discusses pointers in more detail.) In this code, because you're dealing with a reference, you access the object's members using the dot operator (.) rather than the arrow operator (->).

TIP

Another reason to use only pointers and references as parameters for objects is that a function that takes an object as a parameter usually wants to change the object. Such changes require pointers or references.

Using const parameters in functions

A *constant* is a variable or object that another function can't change even when you pass a reference to it to another function. To define a variable or an object as constant, unchangeable, you use the const keyword. For example, to define a variable as constant, you use:

```
const int MyInt = 3;
```

If someone were to come along and try to use the following code:

```
MyInt = 4;
```

The compiler would display an error message saying:

```
error: assignment of read-only variable 'MyInt'
```

The same holds true for a function using a const primitive like this one:

```
void DisplayInt(const int Value) {
    cout << Value << endl;
}
```

It's possible to display Value or interact with it in other ways, but trying to change Value will raise an error. This version will raise an error because Value is being changed:

```
void DisplayInt(const int Value) {
    Value += 1;
    cout << Value << endl;
}
```

The const keyword is useful when working with objects because you generally don't want to pass an object directly. That involves copying the object, which is messy. Instead, you normally pass by using a pointer or reference, which would allow you to change the object. If you put the word const before the parameter, the compiler won't allow you to change the value of the parameter.

REMEMBER

If you have multiple parameters, you can mix const and non-const. If you go overboard, this can be confusing. The following line shows two parameters that are const and another that is not. The function can modify only the members of the object called one.

```
void Inspect(const Pen *Checkitout, Spy *one,
            const Spy *two);
```

Using the this pointer

Consider a function called OneMoreCheeseGone(). It's not a member function, but it takes an object of instance Cheese as a parameter. Its prototype looks like this:

```
void OneMoreCheeseGone(Cheese *Block);
```

This is just a simple function with no return type. It takes an object pointer as a parameter. For example, after you eat a block of cheese, you can call:

```
OneMoreCheeseGone(MyBlock);
```

Now consider this: If you have an object on the heap, it has no name. You access it through a pointer variable that points to it. But what if the code is currently executing inside a member function of an object? How do you refer to the object itself?

C++ has a member variable that exists inside every class: this. It's a pointer variable. The this variable always points to the current object. So, if code execution is occurring inside a member function and you want to call OneMoreCheeseGone(), passing in the current object, you would pass this.

Defining standard this pointer usage

This section tells you how this is used for application development in most applications today. The CheeseClass example, shown in Listing 7-6, demonstrates this.

LISTING 7-6: **Passing an Object from Inside Its Member Functions by Using the this Variable**

```cpp
#include <iostream>

using namespace std;

class Cheese {
public:
  string status;
  void eat();
  void rot();
};

int CheeseCount;

void OneMoreCheeseGone(Cheese *Block) {
  CheeseCount--;
  Block->status = "Gone";
};

void Cheese::eat() {
  cout << "Eaten up! Yummy" << endl;
  OneMoreCheeseGone(this);
}

void Cheese::rot() {
  cout << "Rotted away! Yuck" << endl;
  OneMoreCheeseGone(this);
}

int main() {
    Cheese *asiago = new Cheese();
    Cheese *limburger = new Cheese();
```

```
        CheeseCount = 2;
        asiago->eat();
        limburger->rot();

        cout << endl;
        cout << "Cheese count: " << CheeseCount
            << endl;
        cout << "asiago: " << asiago->status << endl;
        cout << "limburger: " << limburger->status
            << endl;
        return 0;
}
```

The this listing has four main parts. First is the definition for the class called Cheese. The class contains a couple of member functions.

Next is the function OneMoreCheeseGone() along with a global variable that it modifies.

Next come the actual member functions for class Cheese. (You must put these functions after OneMoreCheeseGone() because they call it. If you use a function prototype as a forward reference for OneMoreCheeseGone(), the order doesn't matter.)

Finally, main() creates two new instances of Cheese. When you run the application in Listing 7-6, you see this output:

```
Eaten up! Yummy
Rotted away! Yuck

Cheese count: 0
asiago: Gone
limburger: Gone
```

Take a careful look at the OneMoreCheeseGone() function. It operates on the current object provided as a parameter by setting its status variable to the string Gone. The eat() member function calls it, passing the current object using this. The rot() member function also calls it, again passing the current object via this.

Starting and Ending with Constructors and Destructors

You can add two special member functions to your class that let you provide special startup and shutdown functionality: a *constructor* and a *destructor*. The following sections provide details about these functions.

Starting with constructors

When you create a new instance of a class, you may want to do some basic object setup. Suppose you have a class called Apartment, with a private property called NumberOfOccupants.

When you create a new instance of Apartment, you probably want to start NumberOfOccupants at 0. The best way to do this is by adding a special member function, a *constructor*, to your class. This function has a line of code such as the following:

```
NumberOfOccupants = 0;
```

Whenever you create a new instance of the class Apartment, the computer first calls this constructor for your new object, thereby setting NumberOfOccupants to 0. Think of the constructor as an *initialization function*: The computer calls it when you create a new object.

To write a constructor, you add it as another member function to your class, and make it public. You name the constructor the same as your class. For the class Apartment, you name the constructor Apartment(). The constructor has no return type, not even void. You can have parameters in a constructor (see "Adding parameters to constructors," later in this chapter).

Ending with destructors

When you delete an instance of a class, you may want some *cleanup* code to straighten things out before the object memory is released. For example, your object may have properties that are pointers to other objects. It's essential to delete those other objects. You put cleanup code in a special member function called a destructor. A *destructor* is a finalization function that the computer calls before it deletes your object.

The destructor gets the same name as the class, except it has a tilde (~) at the beginning of it. (The tilde is usually in the upper-left corner of the keyboard.) For a class called Squirrel, the destructor would be ~Squirrel(). The destructor doesn't have a return type, not even void, because you can't return anything from a destructor (the object is gone, after all). You just start with the function name and no parameters. The next section, "Sampling constructors and destructors," shows an example that uses both constructors and destructors.

TIP

Constructors and destructors are a way of life for C++ programmers. Nearly every class has a constructor, and many also have a destructor.

Sampling constructors and destructors

The WalnutClass example, shown in Listing 7-7, uses a constructor and a destructor. This application involves two classes, the main one called Squirrel, which demonstrates the constructor and destructor, and one called Walnut, which is used by the Squirrel class.

LISTING 7-7: **Initializing and Finalizing with Constructors and Destructors**

```
#include <iostream>

using namespace std;

class Walnut {
public:
    int Size;
};

class Squirrel {
private:
    Walnut *MyDinner;
public:
    Squirrel();
    ~Squirrel();
};

Squirrel::Squirrel() {
```

(continued)

LISTING 7-7: *(continued)*

```
      cout << "Starting!" << endl;
      MyDinner = new Walnut;
      MyDinner->Size = 30;
}

Squirrel::~Squirrel() {
   cout << "Cleaning up my mess!" << endl;
   delete MyDinner;
}

int main() {
   Squirrel *Sam = new Squirrel;
   Squirrel *Sally = new Squirrel;

   delete Sam;
   delete Sally;
   return 0;
}
```

The Squirrel class has a property called MyDinner that is a
pointer to a Walnut instance. The Squirrel constructor creates
an instance of Walnut and stores it in MyDinner. The destructor
deletes the instance of Walnut. In main(), the code creates two
instances of Squirrel. Each instance gets its own Walnut to eat.
Each Squirrel creates its Walnut when it starts and deletes the
Walnut when the Squirrel is deleted.

When you run this application, you can see the following lines,
which were spit up by the Squirrel in its constructor and
destructor. (You see two lines of each because main() creates two
squirrels.)

```
Starting!
Starting!
Cleaning up my mess!
Cleaning up my mess!
```

Adding parameters to constructors

A constructor that has no parameters is called the *default
constructor*. But like other member functions, constructors allow

you to include parameters. When you do, you can use these parameters in the initialization process. To use them, you list the arguments inside parentheses when you create the object. Because constructors have parameters, you can create multiple overloaded constructors for a class by varying the number and type of parameters.

Suppose you want the Squirrel class to have a name property. Although you could create an instance of Squirrel and then set its name property, you can specify the name directly by using a constructor. The constructor's prototype looks like this:

```
Squirrel(string StartName);
```

Then, you create a new instance like so:

```
Squirrel *Sam = new Squirrel("Sam");
```

The constructor is expecting a string, so you pass a string when you create the object.

The SquirrelClass example, shown in Listing 7-8, presents an application that includes all the basic elements of a class with a constructor that accepts parameters.

LISTING 7-8: **Placing Parameters in Constructors**

```cpp
#include <iostream>

using namespace std;

class Squirrel {
private:
    string Name;
public:
    Squirrel(string StartName);
    void WhatIsMyName();
};

Squirrel::Squirrel(string StartName) {
    cout << "Starting!" << endl;
    Name = StartName;
```

(continued)

LISTING 7-8:   *(continued)*

```
    }

    void Squirrel::WhatIsMyName() {
        cout << "My name is " << Name << endl;
    }

    int main()
    {
        Squirrel *Sam = new Squirrel("Sam");
        Squirrel *Sally = new Squirrel("Sally");

        Sam->WhatIsMyName();
        Sally->WhatIsMyName();

        delete Sam;
        delete Sally;
        return 0;
    }
```

In `main()`, you pass a string into the constructors. The constructor code takes the `StartName` parameter and copies it to the `Name` property. The `WhatIsMyName()` member function writes `Name` to the console.

You can use a special syntax in a constructor to initialize member variables. For example, you could have written the constructor for class `Squirrel`:

```
    Squirrel::Squirrel(string StartName)
        : Name(StartName)
    {
        cout << "Starting!" << endl;
    }
```

In the constructor header, append a list of the initializations after a colon. Each initialization consists of the member variable name followed by its initial value enclosed in parentheses. If there is more than one initialization, separate them with commas. In the preceding code, by initializing member variable `Name` with the value of parameter `StartName`, you no longer need the assignment statement for `Name`.

Building Hierarchies of Classes

When you start describing classes, you usually discover *hierarchies* of classes. For example, you could divide Vehicle into car brands, such as Ford, Honda, and Toyota. Then you could divide the class Toyota into models, such as Prius, Avalon, Camry, and Corolla. You can create similar groupings of objects for the other class hierarchies; your decision depends on how you categorize things and how the hierarchy is used. In the hierarchy, class Vehicle is at the top. This class has properties you find in every brand or model of vehicle. For example, all vehicles have wheels. How many they have varies, but it doesn't matter at this point, because classes don't have specific values for the properties.

Each brand has certain characteristics that may be unique to it, but each has all the characteristics of class Vehicle. That's called *inheritance*. The class Toyota, for example, has all the properties found in Vehicle. And the class Prius has all the properties found in Toyota, which includes those inherited from Vehicle.

In C++, you can create a hierarchy of classes. When you take one class and create a new one under it, such as creating Toyota from Vehicle, you're *deriving* a new class, which means Toyota is a *child* of Vehicle in the hierarchy.

To derive a class from an existing class, you write the new class as you would any other class, but you extend the header after the class name with a colon (:) the word public, and then the class you're deriving from, as in the following class header line:

```
class Toyota : public Vehicle {
```

When you do so, the class you create (Toyota) *inherits* the member variables and member functions from the *parent* class (Vehicle). For example, if Vehicle has a public member variable called NumberOfWheels and a public member function called Drive(), the class Toyota has these members, although you didn't write the members in Toyota.

The VehicleClass example, shown in Listing 7-9, demonstrates class inheritance. It starts with a class called Vehicle, and a derived class called Toyota. You create an instance of Toyota in main() and call two member functions for the instance,

MeAndMyToyota() and Drive(). The definition of the Toyota class doesn't show a Drive() function. The Drive() function is inherited from the Vehicle class. You can call this function like a member of the Toyota class because in many ways it *is*.

LISTING 7-9:   **Deriving One Class from Another**

```cpp
#include <iostream>

using namespace std;

class Vehicle {
public:
  int NumberOfWheels;

  void Drive() {
    cout << "Driving, driving, driving..."
         << endl;
  }
};

class Toyota : public Vehicle {
public:
  void MeAndMyToyota() {
    cout << "Just me and my Toyota!" << endl;
  }
};

int main() {
  Toyota MyCar;
  MyCar.MeAndMyToyota();
  MyCar.Drive();
  return 0;
}
```

When you run this application, you see the output from two functions:

```
Just me and my Toyota!
Driving, driving, driving...
```

Overriding member functions

The *signature* of a function includes its function name and the number, datatypes, and order of its parameters. (The names of the parameters are not part of the signature.) A subclass can *override* a superclass's member function by defining a member function with the same signature. This allows the subclass to supersede a behavior of its superclass.

In Listing 7-10, class `Item` defines a `print_cost()` member function that prints a regular item's `price` times the `quantity`. You must specify the function to be `virtual` to allow the class's subclasses to override it. When a class has virtual functions, it must also have virtual destructor, even if it only has an empty block:

```
virtual ~Item() {}
```

Subclass `DiscountedItem` has a private `discount`. Its `print_cost()` member function has the same signature, so it overrides `Item`'s function. Its behavior is different because its cost calculation includes a discount. Note the `override` specified in the function header — it must also have a virtual destructor.

Similarly, subclass `DonatedItem`'s `print_cost()` member function overrides `Item`'s member function. It simply prints a 0 cost.

LISTING 7-10: **Overriding Functions**

```cpp
#include <iostream>
#include <string>

using namespace std;

class Item
{
public:
    virtual ~Item() {}

    virtual void print_cost(double price,
                            int quantity)
    {
        cout << "Regular cost = "
```

(continued)

LISTING 7-10:   *(continued)*

```
                    << price*quantity << endl;
        }
};

class DiscountedItem: public Item
{
public:
    DiscountedItem(double d)
        : discount(d) {}

    virtual ~DiscountedItem() {}

    void print_cost(double price,
                    int quantity) override
    {
        cout << "Discounted cost = "
            << price*quantity*(1 - discount)
            << endl;
    }

private:
    double discount;
};

class DonatedItem: public Item
{
public:
    virtual ~DonatedItem() {}

    void print_cost(double price,
                    int quantity) override
    {
        cout << "Donated cost = " << 0 << endl;
    }
};

int main()
{
    Item regular_item;
    DiscountedItem discounted_item(0.25);
    DonatedItem donated_item;
```

```
    regular_item.print_cost(2.99, 3);
    discounted_item.print_cost(2.99, 3);
    donated_item.print_cost(2.99, 3);

    return 0;
}
```

Output from the progam is

```
Regular cost = 8.97
Discounted cost = 6.7275
Donated cost = 0
```

Generating random numbers

The C++ rand() function uses an algorithm to generate *pseudo-random* positive integer values. A program that calls rand() would get the same sequence of pseudo-random values each time it's run. However, you can call function srand() to set a different seed value for the algorithm to get a different sequence. A common seed value is the result of calling the function time(0), which returns the current time in seconds. Then each time you run the program, the seed value is different, so you'll get a different sequence.

Listing 7-11 shows two different ways to get pseudo-random values. Note that you must include cstdlib and ctime.

LISTING 7-11: Pseudo-Random Numbers

```
#include <iostream>
#include <cstdlib>
#include <ctime>

using namespace std;

int main()
{
    srand(time(0));

    for (int i = 0; i < 4; i++)
```

(continued)

LISTING 7-11:	(continued)

```
    {
        cout << " " << rand();
    }
    cout << endl;

    for (int i = 0; i < 4; i++)
    {
        cout << " " << rand()%3;
    }
    cout << endl;

    return 0;
}
```

Each for loop generates and prints four pseudo-random values by calling rand( ). The second for loop uses the % operator to constrain the values to 0, 1, or 2. Example output is as follows:

```
1794106847 735890002 744940541 386010577
 1 0 2 0
```

The call to srand( ) makes the output different each time you run the program.

Using polymorphism

Polymorphism is an important object-oriented programming feature. When a program makes a call on an object's member function at run time, polymorphism dynamically determines which function to call based on which class instantiated the object.

Listing 7-12 shows a modified version of the program in Listing 7-10. Superclass Item and its subclasses DiscountedItem and DonatedItem are unchanged.

LISTING 7-12:	Polymorphism

```
#include <iostream>
#include <cstdlib>
#include <ctime>
```

146 C++ Essentials For Dummies

```cpp
using namespace std;

class Item ...
class DiscountedItem: public Item ...
class DonatedItem: public Item ...

int main()
{
    Item *regular_ptr = new Item;
    DiscountedItem *discounted_ptr =
                    new DiscountedItem(0.25);
    DonatedItem *donated_ptr = new DonatedItem;

    srand(time(0));

    for (int i = 0; i < 10; i++)
    {
        int r = rand()%3;
        cout << r << " ";

        Item *item_ptr;

        switch (r)
        {
            case 0: item_ptr = regular_ptr;
                    break;
            case 1: item_ptr = discounted_ptr;
                    break;
            case 2: item_ptr = donated_ptr;
                    break;
        }

        item_ptr->print_cost(2.99, 3);
    }

    return 0;
}
```

During each iteration of the for loop, the value of variable r can be 0, 1, or 2. Depending on the value of r, the Item pointer variable item_ptr is set to point to an Item, a DiscountedItem, or a DonatedItem object. The pointer variable is able to point to the different objects because `DiscountedItem` and `DonatedItem` objects are instantiated from subclasses of `Item`.

During run time, when the program executes the following statement:

```
item_ptr->print_cost(2.99, 3);
```

The program uses polymorphism to determine which class's `print_cost()` member function to call based on which object `item_ptr` is currently pointing to.

Example output from the program, which will be different during each run, is as follows:

```
0 Regular cost = 8.97
2 Donated cost = 0
0 Regular cost = 8.97
2 Donated cost = 0
1 Discounted cost = 6.7275
1 Discounted cost = 6.7275
2 Donated cost = 0
1 Discounted cost = 6.7275
0 Regular cost = 8.97
0 Regular cost = 8.97
```

In order for the `print_cost()` member functions to behave polymorphically, it must be `virtual` in the superclass and an `override` in each subclass.

Overloading member functions

You can *overload* a member function of a class by defining several versions of it that have similar behaviors. The versions have the same name but different parameters.

Listing 7-13 shows a `Shape` class that overloads its member function `area()`. The different versions of the function compute the areas of various shapes.

LISTING 7-13: **Overloading a Member Function**

```cpp
#include <iostream>
#include <cmath>

using namespace std;

class Shape
{
public:
    double area(double radius)
    {
        return M_PI*radius*radius;
    }

    double area(double width, double height)
    {
        return width*height;
    }

    double area(double length, double width,
            double height)
    {
        return 2*(width*length + height*length
                        + height*width);
    }
};

int main()
{
    Shape circle;
    cout << "area of a circle with radius 2 = "
        << circle.area(2) << endl << endl;

    Shape rectangle;
    cout << "area of a rectangle with width 3"
        << endl;
    cout << "                  and height 4 = "
        << rectangle.area(3, 4) << endl << endl;

    Shape prism;
    cout << "area of a prism with length 3"
```

(continued)

LISTING 7-13: *(continued)*

```
              << endl;
    cout << "                 and width 4"
              << endl;
    cout << "                 and height 5 = "
              << prism.area(3, 4, 5) << endl;

    return 0;
}
```

Only one parameter, the radius, is required to calculate the area of a circle. Two parameters — length and width — are required for a rectangle, and three parameters — length, width, and height — are required for a prism. Therefore, we've overloaded member function area() with one, two, and three parameters.

The output of this program is as follows:

```
area of a circle with radius 2 = 12.5664

area of a rectangle with width 3
                and height 4 = 12

area of a prism with length 3
                and width 4
                and height 5 = 94
```

Chapter **8**

Working with Arrays and Pointers

In this chapter, you encounter the full rundown of topics that lay the foundation for C++: arrays and pointers. In C++, these items come up again and again.

This chapter assumes that you have a basic understanding of C. You know the basics of pointers and arrays and you're ready to grasp them thoroughly. When you finish this chapter, you'll have expanded on your knowledge enough to perform some intermediate and advanced tasks with relative ease.

REMEMBER

The more you know about arrays, the less likely you are to use them incorrectly, which would result in a bug. Know how to get the most out of arrays when necessary — not just because they're there. Avoid using arrays in the most complex way imaginable.

Declaring Arrays

The usual way of declaring an array is to line up the type name, followed by a variable name, followed by a size in brackets, as in this line of code:

```
int Numbers[10];
```

REMEMBER

This code declares an array of ten integers. The first element gets index 0, and the final element gets index 9. Always remember that in C++, arrays start at 0, and the highest index is one less than the size. (*Remember: Index* refers to the position within the array, and *size* refers to the number of elements in the array.)

In certain situations, you can declare an array without putting a number in the brackets. For example, you can initialize an array without specifying the number of elements:

```
int MyNumbers[] = {1,2,3,4,5,6,7,8,9,10};
```

The compiler is smart enough to count how many elements you put inside the braces, and then the compiler makes that count the array size.

Specifying the array size helps decrease your chances of having bugs. Plus, it has the added benefit that, in the actual declaration, if the number in brackets doesn't match the number of elements inside braces, the compiler issues an error. The following

```
int MyNumbers[5] = {1,2,3,4,5,6,7,8,9,10};
```

Yields this compiler error:

```
error: too many initializers for 'int [5]'
```

But if the number in brackets is greater than the number of elements, as in the following code, you won't get an error. Instead, the remaining array elements aren't defined, and if you access them, you'll get whatever values happen to be in memory. So be careful!

```
int MyNumbers[15] = {1,2,3,4,5,6,7,8,9,10};
```

You also can skip specifying the array size when you pass an array into a function, like this:

```
int AddUp(int Numbers[], int Count) {
    int loop;
    int sum = 0;
    for (loop = 0; loop < Count; loop++) {
        sum += Numbers[loop];
    }
```

```
        return sum;
}
```

This technique is particularly powerful because the AddUp() function can work for any size array. You can call the function like this:

```
cout << AddUp(MyNumbers, 10) << endl;
```

But this way to do it is kind of annoying because you have to specify the size each time you call in to the function. However, you can get around this problem. Look at this line of code:

```
cout << AddUp(MyNumbers, sizeof(MyNumbers) /
    sizeof(int)) << endl;
```

Now this line of code works, and here's why: The sizeof the array divided by the sizeof each element in the array gives the number of elements in the array.

Using Arrays and Pointers

The name of the array is a pointer to the array itself. The *array* is a sequence of values stored in memory. The *array name* points to the first item. The following sections discuss arrays and pointers.

When you declare an array by giving a definite number of elements, such as

```
int MyNumbers[5];
```

The compiler knows that you have an array. But if you declare a function header without an array size, such as

```
void ProcessArray(int Numbers[]) {
```

The compiler treats this as simply a *pointer*. This last line is, in fact, equivalent to the following line:

```
void ProcessArray(int *Numbers) {
```

Thus, inside the functions that either line declares, the following two lines of code are *equivalent:*

```
Numbers[3] = 10;
*(Numbers + 3) = 10;
```

REMEMBER Although an array is simply a sequence of values all adjacent to each other in memory, the name of an array is really just a pointer to the first element in the array. You can use the name as a pointer. However, do that only when you really need to work with a pointer. After all, you really have no reason to write code that is cryptic, such as *(Numbers + 3) = 10;.

The converse is also true. Look at this function:

```
void ProcessArray(int *Numbers) {
    cout << Numbers[1] << endl;
}
```

This function takes a pointer as a parameter, yet you access it as an array. Again, don't write code like this.

These tips will help you keep your arrays bug-free:

TIP

>> **Keep your code consistent.** If you declare, for example, a pointer to an integer, don't treat it as an array.

>> **Keep your code clear and understandable.** If you pass pointers, it's okay to take the address of the first element, as in &(MyNumbers[0]) if this makes the code clearer — though it's equivalent to just MyNumbers.

>> **When you declare an array, always try to put a number inside the brackets, unless you're writing a function that takes an array.**

Using Multidimensional Arrays

Arrays don't have to be just one-dimensional. Dimensions make it possible to model data more realistically. For example, a three-dimensional array would allow you to better model a specific place in 3-D space. The following sections discuss using multi-dimensional arrays.

Declaring a multidimensional array

You can declare a multidimensional array using a technique similar to a single-dimensional array, as shown in the Array04 example in Listing 8-1. The difference is that you must declare each dimension separately.

LISTING 8-1: **Using a Multidimensional Array**

```
#include <iostream>

using namespace std;

int MemorizeThis[10][20];

int main() {
    for (int x = 0; x < 10; x++) {
        for (int y = 0; y < 20; y++ ) {
            MemorizeThis[x][y] = x * y;
        }
    }

    cout << MemorizeThis[9][13] << endl;
    cout << sizeof(MemorizeThis) / sizeof(int)
        << endl;
    return 0;
}
```

When you run this, MemorizeThis gets filled with the multiplication table. Here's the output for the application, which is the contents of MemorizeThis[9][13], and then the size of the entire two-dimensional array:

```
117
200
```

And indeed, 9 times 13 is 117. The size of the array is 200 elements. Because each element, being an integer, is 4 bytes, the size of the array in bytes is 800.

You can have many, many dimensions, but be *careful*. Every time you add a dimension, the size multiplies by the size of that dimension.

Considering data type

The data type of your array also makes a difference. Here are some byte values for arrays of the same size, but using different types:

```
char CharArray[20][20];       // 400 bytes
short ShortArray[20][20];     // 800 bytes
long LongArray[20][20];       // 1,600 bytes
float FloatArray[20][20];     // 1,600 bytes
double DoubleArray[20][20];   // 3,200 bytes
```

Initializing multidimensional arrays

Just as you can initialize a single-dimensional array by using braces and separating the elements by commas, you can initialize a multidimensional array with braces and commas, too. But to do this, you combine arrays inside arrays, as in this code:

```
int Numbers[5][6] = {
    {1,2,3,4,5,6},
    {7,8,9,10,12},
    {13,14,15,16,17,18},
    {19,20,21,22,23,24},
    {25,26,27,28,29,30}
};
```

Passing multidimensional arrays

If you have to pass a multidimensional array to a function, things can get just a bit hairy. That's because you don't have as much freedom in leaving off the array sizes as you do with single-dimensional arrays. Suppose you have this function:

```
int AddAll(int MyGrid[5][6]) {
    int x,y;
    int sum = 0;
    for (x = 0; x < 5; x++) {
        for (y = 0; y < 6; y++) {
```

```
    sum += MyGrid[x][y];
  }
 }
 return sum;
}
```

So far, the function header is fine because it explicitly states the size of each dimension. The following code will compile:

```
int AddAll(int MyGrid[][6]) {
```

A multidimensional array is an array of an array. Thus, the compiler treats the statement `MyGrid[5][6]` as if it were `MyGrid[5]` where each item in the array is itself an array of size 6. In an array parameter, you're free not to specify the size of a one-dimensional array. But for subsequent dimensions, you have to give the subarrays *bounds* (a specific number of entries).

TIP

When using multidimensional arrays, it's often easier to think of them as an array of arrays.

Working with Arrays and Command-Line Parameters

In a typical C++ application, the `main()` function receives an array and a count as *command-line parameters* (parameters provided as part of the command to execute that application at the command line). Think of the two parameters as an array of strings and a size of the array. However, each string in this array of strings is actually a character array. The following code from the `CommandLineParams` example shows how you can get the command-line parameters:

```
#include <iostream>

using namespace std;

int main(int argc, char *argv[]) {
  int loop;
  for (loop = 0; loop < argc; loop++) {
```

```
        cout << argv[loop] << endl;
    }
    return 0;
}
```

The first argument is always the name of the executable.

Allocating an Array on the Heap

This section shows how you can allocate an array on the heap by using the new keyword.

You can easily declare an array in the heap by using new int[50], for example. Thus, the call:

```
new int[50]
```

Returns a pointer of type int *.

If you want to save the results of new int [50] in a variable, you have to have a variable of type int *, as in the following:

```
int *MyArray = new int[50];
```

In this case, an array name is a pointer. So, now that you have a pointer to an integer, you can treat it like an array:

```
MyArray[0] = 25;
```

Deleting an Array from the Heap

When you finish using the array on in the heap, you can call delete. The makers of C++ gave us a special form of delete to handle this situation. It looks like this:

```
delete[] MyArray;
```

Chapter **9**

Ten Features for More Advanced C++ Programming

C++ is a large, complex language. To become an expert C++ programmer, you'll need to know much more about the language and its capabilities than this book can cover. This final chapter briefly introduces an additional ten features that will help you become such an expert.

Conditional Compilation

You can use #define along with #ifdef, #else, and #end to do *conditional compilation*, in which you tell the preprocessor which parts of your program the C++ compiler should compile or ignore.

For example, suppose your program calls a function written by another programmer. While debugging your program, you want to know what value the function returns by printing the value. You can write

```
#define DEBUG_FLAG
```

at the start of a source file. Later, when you call the function, you can write

```
    value = mystery(i, j, k);

#ifdef DEBUG_FLAG
    cout << "mystery() is " << value << endl;
#endif
```

Because you had earlier defined DEBUG_FLAG, the preprocessor will include the cout statement for the compiler to compile and, presumably, the statement will execute at run time.

But after you're done debugging your program and you're satisfied with what value mystery() returns, you can remove the #define DEBUG_FLAG. Then the compiler won't see the cout statement, and the function's return value won't be included in the program's output.

Namespaces

A large software project includes many names, and it may involve several programmers. Namespaces can help avoid name conflicts among different parts of the project.

The built-in standard namespace std contains many common names such as cout, cin, string, and vector. To use these names, you can include the statement

```
using namespace std;
```

near the top of a source file. Otherwise, you must use the :: operator every time you use a name in the standard namespace, such as std::cout and std::string.

You can create your own namespaces. The following example header file defines namespace myshapes and the classes that it contains:

```
#ifndef MYSHAPES_H_
#define MYSHAPES_H_

namespace myshapes
```

```
{
    class Shape
    {
        ...
    };

    class Circle : public Shape
    {
        ...
    };

    class Square : public Shape
    {
        ...
    };
}

#endif /* MYSHAPES_H_ */
```

A source file that uses both namespaces std and myshapes needs to be put near the top:

```
using namespace std;
using namespace myshapes;
```

File I/O

C++ uses the concept of *streams* to interface with external files. A *stream* is a sequence of characters that flows between a program and an I/O device. Therefore, to read a file, you first create an input stream and open the file onto the stream. Then you can read values from the input stream. Conversely, to write to a file, you first create an output stream and open the file onto the stream. Then you can write values to the stream.

The following statements create the input file stream ifstream named students_ins, which it opens to read the text file students.txt:

```
#include <iostream>
#include <fstream>
```

```
#include <string>

using namespace std;

int id;
string last, first;

ifstream students_ins;
students_ins.open("students.txt");

students_ins >> id >> last >> first;

students_ins.close();
```

The following statements create the output file stream prices_
outs, which it opens to write to the text file prices.txt:

```
#include <iostream>
#include <fstream>
#include <string>

using namespace std;
. . .
ofstream prices_outs;
prices_outs.open("prices.txt");
. . .
prices_outs << cereal_name << cereal_price
            << endl;
. . .
prices_outs.close();
```

Exception Handling

An *exception* represents a runtime error that your program
can throw when the error occurs. If your program throws an
exception, it must be caught, otherwise the program *aborts*
(abruptly terminates). You write exception handlers with try
catch statements to catch particular exceptions.

The file nonexistent.txt doesn't exist, so the following example program throws an exception when it tries to open the file. The program then catches and handles the exception.

```cpp
#include <iostream>
#include <fstream>
#include <string>

using namespace std;

int main()
{
    string filename = "nonexistent.txt";
    ifstream ins;

    try
    {
        ins.open(filename);
        if (!ins.is_open())
        {
            throw "Failed to open " + filename;
        }

        cout << "Successfully opened "
                + filename << endl;
        ins.close();
    }
    catch (string msg)
    {
        cout << "FILE ERROR: " << msg << endl;
    }

    return 0;
}
```

The output is

```
FILE ERROR: Failed to open nonexistent.txt
```

The code is easier to read if it isn't cluttered with error handlers. So, you can consolidate the error handling statements in catch blocks.

When a program throws an exception, it immediately jumps to the `catch` block. Therefore, in the preceding example, the `Successfully opened` message is not printed.

If the program doesn't catch an exception after it was thrown, it will abort with an error message about an uncaught exception.

REMEMBER

An important feature when throwing an exception in a function is that if the exception isn't caught in that function, the exception propagates up the call chain until a function on the chain, or the main program itself, catches it. If the exception is never caught, the program aborts.

Operator Overloading

C++ allows you to *overload* an operator by giving it an additional capability. For example, you can overload the + operator to define what it means to add two objects of a certain class, and you can overload the << operator to define how to print such an object.

The following example demonstrates overloading the * operator to multiply two fractions and overloading the << operator to print a fraction:

```
#include <iostream>

using namespace std;

class Fraction
{
public:
    Fraction(int n, int d)
        : numerator(n), denominator(d) {}
    int numerator, denominator;
};

Fraction operator *(Fraction& f1, Fraction& f2)
{
    int n = f1.numerator*f2.numerator;
    int d = f1.denominator*f2.denominator;
```

```
        return Fraction(n, d);
}

ostream& operator <<(ostream& outs,
                     const Fraction& f)
{
    float decimal = ((float) f.numerator)
                  / ((float) f.denominator);
    outs << f.numerator << "/" << f.denominator
        << " = " << decimal;
    return outs;
}

int main()
{
    Fraction two_thirds(2, 3);
    Fraction three_fourths(3, 4);

    cout << "   two thirds is "
        << two_thirds << endl;
    cout << "three fourths is "
        << three_fourths << endl;
    cout << "their product is "
        << two_thirds*three_fourths << endl;

    return 0;
}
```

Operator function ∗ overloads the multiplication operator to allow you to multiply two Fraction objects using ∗, as in two_thirds∗three_fourths. The function returns a Fraction object representing the product. Operator function << allows you to output a Fraction object in a desired format in a cout statement. A << operator function always returns a reference to the output stream. That allows chaining the operator in a single cout statement to output multiple values.

The output is

```
   two thirds is 2/3 = 0.666667
three fourths is 3/4 = 0.75
their product is 6/12 = 0.5
```

STL Vectors

The Standard Template Library (STL) is a powerful C++ library of *template classes* that implement data structures such as vectors, hash tables, and iterators. Template classes are models for creating regular classes based on the datatypes that you give them.

For example, vector is a template class, and vector<int> generates a class the implements a sequence of integer values. Similarly, vector<float> generates a class that implements a sequence of float values.

TIP

Vectors are similar to arrays but much more flexible and convenient to use. You can append values to a vector and insert and remove values anywhere in a vector. A vector automatically grows and shrinks its sequence of values.

The following statements demonstrate some of a vector's capabilities. You create a vector<int> object named values, which you initialize to a sequence of integer values 10, 20, and 30.

```
#include <string>
#include <vector>

using namespace std;
...
vector<int> values{10, 20, 30};

// Append a value at the end.
values.push_back(40);

// Insert a value two positions
// from the beginning.
values.insert(values.begin(), 2);
```

STL Maps

A map is an *associative container* that stores key–value pairs. You use a key to access the value associated with the key. A map can't have duplicate keys. You create map classes with the STL map template. For each map, you specify the datatype of the keys and the datatype of the values.

The following statements demonstrate some of a map's capabilities.

```
#include <string>
#include <map>

using namespace std;
...
map<string, int> numbers;

// Add some key-value pairs.
numbers["one"] = 1;
numbers["twenty-one"] = 21;

// Update a pair.
numbers["twenty-one"]++;
```

Variable numbers is a map whose keys are strings, and the associated values are integers. You access each element by using a key like a subscript. So, numbers["one"] = 1 enters the first key-value pair with key "one" and associated value 1. The expression numbers["twenty-one"]++ accesses the element with key "twenty-one" and increments its associated value from 21 to 22.

STL Iterators

An *iterator* is a template class that accesses and iterates through the elements of a sequential template class, such as a vector. A common use is to loop over the elements of the sequence to process each element in turn.

The following statements demonstrate a vector's iterator. The vector of integer values is v, and its iterator is itr. Because the vector's datatype is vector<int>, the iterator's datatype is vector<int>::iterator.

```
#include <vector>
#include <iterator>

using namespace std;
...
vector<int> v{10, 20, 30, 40, 50};
vector<int>::iterator itr;

for (itr = v.begin(); itr != v.end(); itr++)
{
    cout << setw(3) << *iter;
}
cout << endl;

for (int n : v)
{
    cout << setw(3) << n;
}
cout << endl;
```

The first for loop initializes itr to the beginning of the vector, and the loop exits when itr reaches the end of v. The iterator behaves like a pointer. The expression itr++ advances the iterator to the next position of v, and *itr retrieves the element of v at the iterator's current position.

The second for loop implicitly uses the vector's iterator. The first time through the loop, variable n is assigned the value at the first position of v. During each subsequent time through the loop, n is assigned the value at the next position.

There are iterators for the other sequential STL containers and iterators that iterate backward through a sequence.

Algorithms Library

The algorithms library contains functions that perform useful operations, such as sorting and searching. The following example demonstrates functions reverse() and sort() on a vector of strings. The following statements demonstrate reversing the order of the contents of a vector of strings and sorting the strings into alphabetical order.

```
#include <vector>
#include <string>
#include <algorithm>

using namespace std;
...
vector<string> week{"Sunday", "Monday",
                    "Tuesday", "Wednesday",
                    "Thursday", "Friday",
                    "Saturday"};

reverse(week.begin(), week.end());

sort(week.begin(), week.end());
```

Smart Pointers

A common runtime error when using *raw* (regular) pointers is forgetting to delete dynamically created objects that the pointers are pointing to. That can cause the heap to become filled with objects that the program no longer uses. Another common error is to attempt to delete an object more than once.

WARNING

Even if an object in the heap has been deleted by executing a `delete` statement with the pointer variable, the variable is not automatically set to `nullptr`, and it still points to the memory where the object used to be. That can cause hard-to-detect logic errors.

C++ now has "smart" pointers that alleviate the problems caused by raw pointers. There are two kinds of smart pointers: *unique pointers* and *shared pointers*.

A unique pointer has exclusive ownership of the object it points to. No other smart pointer can also point to that object, but the ownership can be transferred to another unique pointer by using `std::move()`. After such a transfer, the original owner pointer is automatically set to `nullptr`. The object pointed to by a unique pointer is automatically deleted when the unique pointer goes out of scope, such as upon return from a function where the unique pointer was declared.

The following statements demonstrate unique pointers. When declaring a unique pointer, you can initialize it with a raw pointer or with `nullptr`. You can use the unique pointer's `reset()` method to change its value. You can access the value pointed to by a smart pointer with `*` and `->` as you would with a regular pointer.

```
using namespace std;
...
unique_ptr<Item> uniq_ptr1(new Item(101));
unique_ptr<Item> uniq_ptr2(nullptr);

uniq_ptr2 = std::move(uniq_ptr1);
uniq_ptr2.reset(new Item(888));
cout << uniq_ptr2->id;
```

An object in the heap can be pointed to by multiple shared pointers; these pointers have shared ownership of the object. The object is automatically deleted when the last of its shared pointers no longer points to the object. So, the object is deleted only once.

The following statements create shared pointers:

```
shared_ptr<Item> shar_ptr1(new Item(101));
shared_ptr<Item> shar_ptr2(shar_ptr1);
```

Index

A

accessing members, 126–128

adding
- header files, 85
- integer variables, 16–19
- onto strings, 28
- parameters to constructors, 138–140
- two strings, 28–29

AddOne( ) function, 130

addresses, for variables, 97–98

AddUp( ) function, 153

algorithms library, 168–169

alias, 131

allocating
- arrays on heaps, 158
- memory on the heap, 107

angle brackets, using in header files, 85–86

Apple macOS, using C++ on, 5–6

application flow
- about, 37
- break statement, 54–55
- continue statement, 54, 55–56
- decision-making using conditional operator, 45–46
- evaluating conditions in C++, 39–42
- filling code with comments, 37–39
- for loop, 47–51
- nested loops, 56–57
- repeating actions with looping statements, 47
- switch statements, 57–60

using if statements and conditions, 42–44

while loop, 51–54

area( ) function, 148–150

array variables, 10

arrays
- about, 78, 107, 151
- allocating on heaps, 158
- command-line parameters and, 157–158
- declaring, 151–153
- deleting from heaps, 158
- multidimensional, 154–157
- pointers and, 153–154

arrow operator (=>), 109, 128–129, 132

ASCII table, 23

assignment statement, 12, 40

associative containers, 166–167

asterisk (*), 20, 101, 106, 114

B

backslash (\), 25

behaviors, 118–119, 125

Boolean variables
- about, 29–30
- conditional operators and, 46

break statement, 54–55

C

C++
- advanced features of, 159–170
- evaluating condition in, 39–42

D

data
  referring to through pointers, 95–116
  storing in C++, 9–36
data type, 156
deallocate, 105
debugger, 8
decision-making, using conditional operators, 45–46
declaring
  arrays, 151–153
  character variables, 24
  multidimensional arrays, 155–156
  multiple variables, 12–13
  variables (*See* variable declaration)
decrement operator, 20, 50
decrementing the variable, 20
default constructor, 138
#define, creating constants with, 93
delete operator, 109
deleting arrays from heaps, 158
dereferencing, 95, 107
destructors
  ending with, 136–137
  sampling, 137–138
directives, 91–93
dividing
  integer variables, 21–23
  work with functions, 61–63
dot operator (.), 132
double quotes (""), 25
double slash (\\), 38
double values, printing, 31–33
do–while loop, 47
dynamic memory management, 105

E

Eclipse CDT, 7
else keyword, 43–44
ending, with destructors, 136–137
enumerations, 33–34
equal to (==) operator, 40
erase() function, 76–77
evaluating conditions in C++, 39–42
exception handling, 162–164
exponent, 30
extraction operator (>>), 35

F

fabs() function, 62, 63–64, 65
filling code with comments, 37–39
float values, printing, 31–33
float variable, 30
floating point, 10
floating-point numbers
  about, 10
  using in variables, 30–31
for loop
  about, 47
  performing, 48–50
forward references, 72–73, 119
fourth position, 27
freeing pointers, 108–111
function prototypes, 72–73, 80–81, 119
functions
  about, 61
  calling, 63–66
  calling string, 76–77
  dividing work, 61–63
  forward references, 72–73
  function prototypes, 72–73
  initialization, 136

L

length, for variable names, 16
length( ) function, 103
less than (<) operator, 40
less than or equal to (<=) operator, 40
linkage editor, 5
Linux, using C++ on, 6–7
local variables, 70–72
logical operators, 42
loops, nested, 56–57

M

magnitude, 30
main( ) function, 11, 26, 63, 66, 71,
    72–73, 75, 77–78, 79, 99,
    112–113, 114, 116, 126, 128,
    135, 138, 140, 157
member functions
    overloading, 148–150
    overriding, 143–145
    separating code, 119–124
members, accessing, 126–128
memory leaks, creating, 96
Microsoft Visual C++, 7
Microsoft Windows, using C++ on, 4–5
minus minus (--), 20
modulus operator (%), 16, 22
Mueller, John Paul (author)
    C++ All-in-One For Dummies, 1
multidimensional arrays, 154–157
multiplying integer variables, 20–21

N

names
    creating for variables, 15–16
    of variables, 10
namespaces, 160–161

nested loops, 56–57
new, 106, 107
newline character (\n), 24
nonprintable characters, 24–25
not equal to (!=) operator, 39, 40
null character, 24

O

objects
    about, 61, 117–118
    classifying, 118
    defined, 125
    passing to functions, 130–132
operands, 17
operators
    conditional, 45–46
    logical, 42
    overloading, 164–165
    relational, 40–41
or (| |) operator, 41–42
output, 62
overloading
    about, 74–75
    member functions, 148–150
    operators, 164–165
overriding member functions, 143–145

P

parameters
    about, 66
    adding to constructors, 138–140
    using multiple, 67–69
    using no, 67–69
parent class, 141
passing
    multidimensional arrays, 156–157
    multiple variables, 65–66

About the Author

John Mueller was a freelance author and technical editor. He had writing in his blood — he produced more than 100 books and more than 600 articles, on topics ranging from networking to artificial intelligence and from database management to heads-down programming. John provided technical editing services to various magazines and his technical editing skills helped more than 70 authors refine their manuscripts. He also performed various kinds of consulting and wrote certification exams. Read more about John at www.johnmuellerbooks.com.

About the Editor

Ronald Mak teaches computer science and data science at San Jose State University in California's Silicon Valley. He has written books on software design, compiler construction, and numerical computing. He was formerly a senior scientist at NASA and JPL, a research staff member at IBM Research, and an enterprise software specialist at the Lawrence Livermore National Laboratory. Earlier in his career, he held senior software engineering positions at Hewlett-Packard, Sun Microsystems, and Apple. Read more about Ron at www.cs.sjsu.edu/~mak.

Publisher's Acknowledgments

Executive Editor: Lindsay Berg
Editor: Elizabeth Kuball
Proofreader: Debbye Butler

Production Editor:
Tamilmani Varadharaj
Cover Design and Image: Wiley